Decoding Bollywood

Sonia Golani has a BA (Hons.) in History from Lady Shri Ram College and a Masters degree from the University of Delhi. An entrepreneur, she manages her firm, Management Consultants Group which specializes in recruitment of professionals (MBAs and CAs) for Banking, Financial Services, Insurance and FMCG sectors.

She had the distinction of securing a second rank in Rajasthan State in class X Board exams. Later while pursuing ISC from Maharani Gayatri Devi Girl's School, she topped her school. In college, she was elected as Treasurer, Students' Union.

Her second book, *My Life, My Rules: Stories of 18 Unconventional Careers* was published to much acclaim in 2013. Passionate about life and its nuances, she plans to write several books, play golf, help people make better careers for themselves – and hopefully do all of this with equal fervour!

Praise for *My Life, My Rules: Stories of 18 Unconventional Careers*

"At the outset, let me congratulate you on bringing out an inspiring and very important book - *My Life, My Rules* (though what made me pick it up a couple of days ago was the catch phrase: *Stories of 18 Unconventional Careers*). ... Please do keep writing and continue to do so in the easy, free-flowing style that you have."—Subramanian Kalpathi, | Associate Partner, Memcorp Learning and Performance Solutions

"Good Read. I thoroughly enjoyed reading this book. Very inspirational. Learned a lesson that age, education is not a barrier if one decides to do something." – Akhila, on Flipkart

"A must buy for everyone…students, professionals, women, aspiring entrepreneurs, businessmen, etc.…just on the last couple of chapters of this book.…the author has done a great job and picked right people which perfectly matches the title of this book." Gaurav, on Flipkart

"A good book is one that makes you think. You read it for a while. Some lines of it strike a chord inside you and you sit thinking about the lines and the ripples it created within you. You start reading the rest. Some line hits you. You start thinking again. This happens over and over until you finish the book. It was really rare that you find such books." – Bhanu, on Goodreads

"Reading your book…*My Life, My Rules*…Great…want to meet." – Kavita Seth, playback singer

SONIA GOLANI

Westland Ltd

westland ltd

61, Silverline Building, Alapakkam Main Road, Maduravoyal, Chennai 600 095
No. 38/10 (New No.5), Raghava Nagar, New Timber Yard Layout, Bangalore 560026
93, 1st Floor, Sham Lal Road, Daryaganj, New Delhi 110 002

First published by westland ltd 2014

Copyright © Sonia Golani 2014
Illustrations copyright © Ahlawat Gunjan 2014

10 9 8 7 6 5 4 3 2 1

ISBN: 978-93-84030-30-8
Typeset: PrePSol Enterprises Pvt. Ltd.

**For
Mr M. V. Golani
(1931-2013)**

We miss you Papa; You will live forever, in our hearts!

Contents

Acknowledgements

To Dilip Golani, my husband and Varun, my son: I don't have the slightest hesitation in reiterating many times over that it's a true blessing to have you both in my life. Thanks for all your love and encouragement, Dilip and for letting me follow my heart and instinct. You are the rock, I am like the waves; your ocean-like serenity, the perfect foil to my swirling temperament.

Varun, my son, I am so proud to be your mother! I see the making of a man in you, having the same dedication and clarity of thought like your father. I draw my energy and motivation from you and Dilip and all that I wish for is God's blessings to keep this circle of positive energy going.

My parents, H C Motwani and Subhash Motwani from whom I learn what everlasting companionship means and what good parenting is all about. I fall back on you for inspiration all the time, mom and dad!

My mother-in-law, Radha Golani for whose unconditional love for the family, I have immense admiration. The unflinching care she gave to my father-in-law, M V Golani for long years before he passed away in August 2013, makes me bow to her and put her on a pedestal. She is a true beacon of inspiration for us all.

To all my family members and friends whose endless love and support and the entertaining exchanges through all the possible mediums bring so much energy, vitality and the most valued zing to life: Madhavi & Anil Advani, Prashant, Priya, Vikram & Muskaan Motwani, Ashok, Madhavi, Mahesh & Bhavana Golani, Tara & Anil Ruchandani, Pushpa & Jai Vidhani, Anupam & Shubhra Verma, Jyoti & Sanjeev Singh, Rajiv & Sangeeta Sabharwal, Aparna & Maninder Juneja, Manjiri & Girish Kamat, Sonia Gauba, Harsharan Sabharwal, Disha Nawani, Arti Punjabi, Ame Rungta, Nivedita Goel Agarwala, Priti Singh, Priya Singh Aggarwal, Deeptha Venkatadari, Vandana Modi, Kusum Suresh, Reenu

& Praveen Sharma, Devyani & Vivek Sehgal, Arti & Vivek Sood… – life seems so exciting with you all there ☺ Thanks for making it so beautiful!!

My deepest gratitude to all the participants in the book for sharing their precious time and experiences with me wholeheartedly. A special mention for Mahesh Bhatt and Prakash Jha for their affability and graciousness which helped the book to get a wonderful start.

I can never thank you enough Mahesh ji, Prakash ji, Rakeysh, Ashutosh, Rohit, Balki, Anurag, Farah, Zoya, Kunal, Nagesh, Nandita, Vipul, Kabir and Sudhir ji for taking me on a journey through your lives. I will cherish the interactions forever and I do hope that we'll meet again at different points in our journeys as they unfold from here on.

Tani Basu, Naresh Tandon, Srikant Velagaleti – sincere thanks for all your support!

Thanks, Jaideep Varma—your film, *Baawra Mann* on Sudhir Mishra gave a good glimpse into his life.

Amarjeet, Mr. Nair, Sanobar at Lowe Lintas, Sunita at Kromakay, Harshit, Preksha, Aashin Shah and Sujata Jadhav from NCPA – thank you!

Thank you team Westland: Sudha Sadanand, the Managing Editor without whose conviction in the concept, this book would not have become a reality.

Gunjan Ahlawat & Nitesh Mohanty for designing the beautiful cover and sketches for this book as well as for my earlier book, *My Life, My Rules: Stories of 18 Unconventional Careers.*

Anushree, Sarita, Avani, Satish, Krishna Kumar, Rajaram, Navin, Sankar, Gururaj, Satheesh for your incredible support.

Last but not the least, THANK YOU Gautam Padmanabhan, the captain of the ship, for inspiring the team to remain so driven, motivated, warm and friendly which makes every interface with Westland a pure joy!

Author's Note

It gives me great pleasure to present my third book, *Decoding Bollywood: Stories of 15 Film Directors*. After having written about two themes close to my heart viz., "women in leadership positions" covered in my first book, *Corporate Divas* and "following your heart" covered in the second, *My Life, My Rules: Stories of 18 Unconventional Careers*, I decided to write a book on Bollywood, the most popular name for the Mumbai film industry (even though unacceptable to many), which touches the lives of millions through one way or the other.

I am one of those millions of Indians who grew up watching Hindi movies: from the iconic *Sholay*, when I must have been about six years old, to *Satte Pe Satta*; *Qayamat Se Qayamat Tak* in my teens; *Bhaag Milkha Bhaag* recently; art house cinema like *Arth* and *Saaransh*; and evergreen classics like *Awara*, *Mother India*, *Mughal-e-Azam*, *Aradhana* and *Anand*. I reckon most of us would concede that you can't live in India and be oblivious to either Bollywood and cricket, the two main pillars of entertainment which continue to obsess the nation. That I am a resident of Mumbai, the film capital of the country, was another compelling reason to write a book on this subject. Coincidentally, 2013 commemorating the centenary year of Indian cinema, also made it the most opportune time to have a book of this kind.

As the title suggests, *Decoding Bollywood: Stories of 15 Film Directors* is essentially an account of my interactions with some of Bollywood's most prominent directors. Considering the timelines, logistics and the framework of the book, fifteen directors have been covered in this edition from several others who have undoubtedly made significant contribution to Indian cinema.

These stories are not meant to offer a critique of the directors' films; my attempt is to delve into the professional and personal journeys of fifteen filmmakers in order to unravel and decode some aspects of the Hindi film industry. Amongst several other things, my conversations explore the creative world inhabited by some of the most talented minds in the world of cinema; their insights and learnings of the business; Bollywood's elusive quest for the Oscars; the use of marketing blitzkrieg for a film's success, professional ethics and so on.

It is my belief that the best way to understand the world around us is through conversations with people who walk this beautiful planet with us as co-travellers. One to one conversations make the world come alive in a more humane way and help make better and deeper sense of our surroundings, cutting out the clutter and noise of information overload, where many a time the more significant aspects related to individuals tend to get lost. It is to capture this understanding, sans the glitz, that I follow the conversation format and write the books I do.

I have personally known several people who were attracted by the glamour of the film industry and at some point had either wanted to become film stars or filmmakers. But most of them knew very little about the dynamics of the film world that existed in Mumbai. Today, even though Bollywood-related information occupies a lot of space in newsprint and the electronic media, there are perhaps very few books that give a glimpse into what it entails to achieve success in the tinsel town. It is therefore my attempt to present a cohesive picture of the industry through the stories of these filmmakers—directors, who are in more ways than one captains of their ships, the bosses on the film set. The story of each director brings out some interesting facts and nuances of the industry and that in my view is the key take away from the book for every reader, those who seek a breakthrough in the industry or are simply interested in films and its world.

My close interactions with these creators of cinematic magic broght home several facts—why a particular director makcs the kind of movies he or she does; often, how movies reflect the persona of a director; their take on life; point of view on a subject which is quite often drawn from their respective milieus and so on.

While writing this book, one significant aspect that became conspicuous about Bollywood is how production houses in Mumbai work more like family enterprises and many of the key players of the industry are actually related to each other. This is best defined by the Chopra-Johar clan. The late B R Chopra who directed and produced memorable films like *Naya Daur* (1957) and the television serial, *Mahabharat* (1988), had set up his production house in Mumbai in the late Forties which is now run by his son, Ravi Chopra. B R Chopra's younger brother, the late Yash Chopra founded the powerhouse Yash Raj Films in the early Seventies, now managed by his son, Aditya Chopra. Hiroo 'Chopra' Johar, mother of Karan Johar who runs the highly successful Dharma Productions is B R and Yash Chopra's youngest sister. These relationships bring out a certain facet of the industry and a reference to this aspect is in no way meant to undermine the talent and abilities of different individuals who despite filial connections, have shone out on the strength of their own abilities.

It was interesting when I learnt that the internationally acclaimed film director, Shekhar Kapur is legendary actor Dev Anand's sister's son. Or that Farah Khan's mother, Menka 'Irani' Khan and Salman Khan's father, Salim Khan were cast as the lead pair in one of the films in the early Sixties, produced by Menka's mother. Padmini Kolhapure, a popular actress of the Eighties and aunt of Shraddha Kapoor of *Aashiqui 2* fame, is related to the Mangeshkar clan and so on and so forth. Through the stories of Zoya Akhtar, Farah Khan, Rohit Shetty and Mahesh Bhatt in this book, the readers get a perspective of those who come from film families and have deep roots in the industry. Yes, clans and kinships do exist but what's heartening and uplifting about the Mumbai film world is an innate respect for talent irrespective of connections or well-embedded "roots". Over the years, the industry has embraced many, who started from scratch but had the requisite talent, a fire in the belly and a deep desire to achieve, by bestowing them with unparalleled fame and success.

This book also covers stories of directors who came from an academically oriented background to Mumbai to pursue their dreams and made their way to the top with no previous industry connections, whatsoever. Prakash Jha and Sudhir Mishra, featured in this book, owe their success in some measure to the training imparted by the Film and Television Institute of India or FTII (even though Prakash did not complete the course and Sudhir was not even on its rolls) and the National Film Development Corporation of India (NFDC). What is remarkable about their stories is both began by being associated with parallel cinema in the late Eighties and managed to make a successful transition to mainstream, contemporary cinema.

During the writing of this book, I discovered how most filmmakers ascribed the desire to make films as some sort of a compulsion, an uncontrollable urge that made them give up their regular professions to be able to tell stories. The book covers advertising professionals like R Balki and Rakeysh Omprakash Mehra, documentary filmmaker Kabir Khan and actor Nandita Das, who yielded to their strong inner calling, leveraged their experiences and succeeded in making outstanding films. Nagesh Kukunoor, a post graduate from the Georgia Institute of Technology in Atlanta, gave up a promising career in the United States to come back to India and follow his passion to be a filmmaker.

It also became apparent how Indian television and theatre made significant contributions to Bollywood. If the television of the late Eighties catapulted Shah Rukh Khan to

Mumbai, it is because of television in the liberalized Nineties, that directors like Anurag Basu, Kunal Kohli and Vipul Shah were able to secure a place in the directors' roll of honour! Television came to the rescue of Ashutosh Gowariker when he needed to take a break from films to later return with a bang. It was again television which provided a strong base for successful corporate studios like UTV Motion Pictures to emerge as a strong player in films.

Even as the traditional model of operating production houses continues, the major players in this segment being Yash Raj Films (Aditya Chopra), Dharma Productions (Karan Johar), Balaji Telefilms (Ekta Kapoor), Vishesh Films (the Bhatts), Red Chillies Entertainment (Shah Rukh Khan), Aamir Khan Productions, Excel Entertainment (Farhan Akhtar), Filmkraft (Rakesh Roshan), the trend is now veering towards co-production by two or more production houses alongwith corporates in order to share costs, minimize risks and encourage financial transparency. Corporatization has also resulted in reducing the apparent chaos in the industry and led to a tidy division of labour where the directors can completely focus on scripts, content and direction, while the studio (prominent ones being Disney UTV, Eros, Viacom 18, YRF, Reliance Entertainment, Fox Star, etc) takes care of funding, marketing, promotion, distribution and exhibition, taking a huge burden off the shoulders of creative professionals.

The Indian film industry is flourishing at a robust double digit growth rate per annum and is expected to grow at an even higher rate, particularly with newer markets opening up overseas due to a large fan base amongst the Indian diaspora and even non-Indians. As Indian cinema completes hundred years and steps into the next century, it's indeed a great time and place to be when there is a virtual collapse of cultural boundaries between nations. Indian actors, musicians and technicians are actively participating in cross border projects and garnering considerable appreciation. While we are one of the oldest and largest film industries in the world, it is time for the Indian film industry to step up and be reckoned for its quality at an international level while it continues to win the hearts of more than a billion countrymen at home.

I'd say it's a delicate but not an impossible task for the industry that is brimming with confidence, and seems flushed with resources!

Sonia Golani

THE UNPRETENTIOUS BRAVEHEART

ANURAG BASU

Anurag Basu comes across as a man who is completely unpretentious, perfectly comfortable in his own skin, and someone who laughs easily.

I meet him at his editing office in Malad which is located on the top floor of a seven-storey residential apartment in a bylane opposite Inorbit Mall, a popular shopping destination in suburban Mumbai. As I gather later, it's routine for stars like Ranbir Kapoor, Priyanka Chopra, Ileana D' Cruz, Kangana Ranaut, and the likes to hang out here when they are either working or partying with Anurag. The place has a very earthy feel to it with no unnecessary interventions by interior decorators. A four feet, white clay idol of Goddess Saraswati, dressed in the traditional Bengali-style sari, is at the centre of the room – as if to bless and inspire artists to achieve excellence in their crafts.

Anurag arrives for the meeting from his residence close by at Goregaon, instructs his staff briefly before choosing a bean bag for comfort and the conversation that is to follow between us.

Born in the steel township of Bhilai, Anurag and his younger brother were raised like other middle class children with a focus on academics. Anurag's father, Subroto Bose worked with the Steel Authority of India Limited (SAIL) and his mother, Deepshikha taught at the township school. Along with their routine jobs, the Boses ran an amateur theatre group called Abhiyaan which filled their otherwise dreary life with some excitement.

'After a full day's work at the Plant, theatre was like a breath of fresh air for my parents. All my childhood memories are around this theatre group. Every evening, at least thirty cups of tea were made at our home and the only task my brother and I had was to serve chai to troupe members. I used to look forward to the evenings. I saw my dad direct plays and that perhaps helped me later as a filmmaker,' recalls Anurag.

Along with the kids, Abhiyaan also grew and occasionally even travelled to other states. However, the boys were discouraged by their parents to take up theatre as the scope for it, they felt, was limited especially in a place like Bhilai. Therefore the Bose kids didn't think of a career beyond engineering or medicine!

When Anurag was in the tenth grade, his father was invited by the renowned filmmaker, Shyam Benegal to Mumbai during the making of the historical docu-drama, *Bharat Ek Khoj: The Discovery of India* for Doordarshan. Subroto was instantly mesmerized by Mumbai, a world inhabited by artists and on his return to Bhilai, expressed his wish to relocate to Mumbai, to his wife. Being a fellow artist, Deepshikha wasn't in the least perturbed by the sudden turn of events, and went along with his decision. Encouraged by her support, even though he had a couple of service years left, Subroto opted for voluntary retirement and left for Mumbai to try his luck in the city of dreams.

Anurag, however, was not very happy with his father's decision. 'My parents were dreamers… but I couldn't understand it at that age and wondered why my father was leaving for Mumbai? My friends would taunt me often, saying, *"Tera baap hero banne gaya hai* (Your father has gone to become a hero)." I didn't know how to tell them, *"Hero banne nahin gaye hain* (He has not gone to become a hero); he will do theatre and write"; he wanted to become a writer,' he shares.

Even as Subroto struggled to find work and establish himself in Mumbai, Anurag focused on academics and made it through the Pre-Engineering Test and got admission into the Jabalpur Engineering College. But by then, the latent creative impulses in him had fully flowered. His talent as a writer and director was evident through his involvement in theatre, both in school and elsewhere. Gradually, he came to appreciate and relate to his parents' dream and somewhere inside him too, a desire had taken root to be in Mumbai. He confessed to his parents that he didn't want to pursue engineering and would rather do something related to the entertainment industry, which they instantly supported. Anurag then thought of joining the Film and Television Institute (FTII) in Pune, but the minimum qualification required for it was graduation. He promptly therefore enrolled himself in a Physics (Hons) course at the Royal College, in Dahisar, Mumbai.

This step heralded a major transition phase for the Basu family. Deepshikha also quit her job in Bhilai and finally shifted to Mumbai. After a comfortable life in the quaint steel-city, the Basus chose to live in a one BHK (Bedroom, Hall, Kitchen) apartment in the far off suburb of Dahisar.

'If we had continued to stay in Bhilai, I would have been my father's shadow, but in Mumbai, I could do my own thing ,' says Anurag. He wasted no time and formed a theatre group with his collegemates which participated in several inter-college festivals, considered extremely prestigious in Mumbai, and stood first in several such competitions by defeating leading colleges of the city.

However, whenever he travelled with his theatre group, his father would advise him, '*Natak mein "na atak"* (Don't get stuck in theatre),' as he had struggled as a theatre artist in the city. 'Once I began looking for work, I started loving him more and doubly appreciated the pains he had taken for all of us,' acknowledges Anurag and continues, 'I had to earn a living as I realized that I could not burden my family with expenses for my education. Therefore, from the very first year in college, I began working in the film industry and also because I wanted to understand the world of films. All of us in the family were struggling as there wasn't any permanent source of income. I would sit outside many offices to get work, with no Godfather or anyone to encourage me!'

After several such attempts, Anurag landed a role in a play at Prithvi Theatre where he met a lot of aspiring actors. On one such day while he was rehearsing at Prithvi, Prakash Mehra Productions was holding auditions in nearby Juhu. Anurag managed to bag a role as one of the hero's four friends, which included 2-3 lines of dialogue and 500 rupees per day!

'I didn't tell anyone at home and decided to do this miniscule role. Before that, I had also tried to get a job as an assistant director, but that didn't work out. More of such tiny roles came my way. I remember, during the filming of a dance sequence, with the hero in a paddy field, I asked one of the background dancers how much he got paid and was told he made 800 bucks! I made friends with him and started looking for dancing roles which drew better remuneration.'

When I hear this from Anurag, I feel quite amused to imagine him as a dancer. I ask him whether he dances well and learn that he is not only a good dancer but has also choreographed all the song sequences in his movies! He then points out to me how his films never carry any end credits for a choreographer!

Meanwhile, Anurag's entire focus remained on being *present* on a film set. As was obvious, his final objective was to wield the director's baton, but since that seemed far fetched, he even assisted make-up artist, Malay Dasgupta for some time. Gradually, Anurag came to realize that the film industry was a tough and insecure terrain and decided that after his graduation, he would give himself a few more months to test the waters, or else give up on his celluloid dream.

This was around the early Nineties when the satellite television boom had revolutionized the electronic media sector and getting a job in television had become far easier than a break in cinema. As luck would have it, Anurag also landed a job in television as an assistant director with Raman Kumar and Vinta Nanda's production company, Tracinema albeit on a meagre salary, a major part of which the senior assistants would bully him into spending on them. Soon an opportunity came up with Zee TV Network and driven by a strong urge "to gallop" ahead, he crossed over and was assigned the task of making pilot episodes. At that time, although many production houses were making pilots by the dozen, they invariably lay in shelves and never got made into full-fledged series and therefore after several such experiences, Anurag finally also quit Zee.

Meanwhile, Karuna Samtani who was then the Programming Head at Zee, was impressed with Anurag's work and recommended him to Raman Kumar for the position of director with Tracinema! 'Raman Kumar didn't realize that the guy Karuna was recommending was once his assistant because he never took notice of me when I was working with him. He used to usually address me as, "*ae ladke* (you boy)".... I was a nameless unit hand!' recounts Anurag.

So here he was, back at Tracinema but with better luck this time. During his second stint, bypassing senior members, Anurag was once asked to direct an entire scene for the iconic series, *Tara* and soon thereafter, was given the responsibility of directing an entire episode, followed by the complete series! And gradually, there came a time when Anurag Basu became synonymous with some of the most successful soap operas on Indian television.

By now, his parents had also become an integral part of his team. Even as early as his first stint with Tracinema, Anurag had launched his own production company called, Deepshikha Productions, after his mother's name (which was later relaunched as Ishana Productions after his elder daughter's name).

Anurag and his father began by producing their first pilot episode independently and took a huge risk by investing all their hard-earned money, amounting to a couple of lakhs, into the project. Unfortunately, the pilot found no approval and was canned. Anurag had learnt one of his first harsh lessons from this bitter experience and as a result of which, even when he had a steady and successful second stint with Tracinema, followed by Ekta Kapoor's Balaji Telefilms, he kept his work diversified and continued to undertake freelance work for his production house. 'All the members of my family were involved in the world of films – I was assisting, my mother was managing a dubbing unit, my father was writing and directing and my younger brother who was then studying, later became a cameraman. Even though we were in a small house and in a new world, we were happy and Mumbai felt like the right place to be,' reflects Anurag.

For the Basus, the good phase lasted for nearly six years during which Anurag scaled the pinnacle of success in the tv industry; not only was he paid fabulously, he directed all the pilots for some of the most popular and successful shows like *Kyunki Saas Bhi Kabhi Bahu Thi*, *Kahani Ghar Ghar Ki* and the much acclaimed, *Koshish Ek Asha*, etc.

Although everything was going very well and he had the three essentials for a success story in Mumbai namely, name, fame and money, for the first time since he had started work in the industry, he began to feel stagnated with the routine, '*Sab kuch boring lag raha tha* (Everything seemed boring).' His enthusiasm of going to a set began waning and he often waited to hear himself shout—Pack up! Even as he was convincing himself that he should move away from the daily rigour of tv soaps, an exciting opportunity came up in the shape of a documentary called, *Distant Thunder*, on the problems of insurgency in the North-East with Raman Kumar, through the Voluntary Health Association Of India or VHAI . The project gave Anurag the much needed excitement – meeting members of the separatist outfit, ULFA, a few "underground" AASU leaders and investigating the death of an NGO worker – and most importantly, falling in love with Tani, who was part of the VHAI team in Guwahati!

On his return to Mumbai however, the same feeling of ennui resurfaced and he decided to stop working altogether. He was afterall at the height of his career in television and had managed to save enough for his survival. Meanwhile, his employer, Ekta Kapoor of Balaji Telefilms learnt of his decision and offered him his first break in films. This enthused Anurag to such an extent that alongwith the film, he also resumed directing tv shows! But very soon, he realized that as far as television was concerned, he had enjoyed a great professional relationship based on mutual respect and creative independence with Ekta, but when it came to the film, it was different. As early as the first schedule of the film, their differences became apparent and the relationship was severely strained. Anurag left the film mid way, knowing full well that abandoning his first film might close the option of filmmaking forever.

He once again went back to fulltime television, and begAn working on a show with the now-defunct, Plus Channel which had a fairly large set up at that time. Amongst others, the famous director Mahesh Bhatt was also a partner in the company and one day impressed with Anurag's talent, sprung a surprise on him by asking him to meet his brother, Mukesh Bhatt at Vishesh Films. But the experience did not turn out to be particularly encouraging for Anurag because when he went to Vishesh's office, then located in Juhu, he saw Mahesh and Mukesh in deep discussion with their "in house" directors, Vikram Bhatt and Tanuja Chandra, etc., and they barely paid any attention to him.

Sometime later, Anurag accidentally met Mahesh Bhatt at the Delhi airport and heard the same thing from the maverick director, '*Aao, aakey milo mere office mein* (Come and meet me in my office).' In spite of his earlier experience, Anurag was undeterred and thought, '*Chalo, chalte hain* (Let's go and meet).' This time around, Mahesh Bhatt was alone in his office and straightaway came to the point, '*Koi subject hai?* (Do you have any subject for a film?)' Anurag answered flatly, '*Pehli film karni shuru ki thi, woh toh band ho gayi aur tab se film ke baare mein sochna bhi band kar diya hai* (I started working on my first film but after it got stalled, I have stopped thinking about films).' Mahesh Bhatt then offered to send him a script, which he promptly did the next day. This was the script for Anurag's first film with the Bhatts—a romantic-horror mystery called *Saaya*, starring John Abraham and Tara Sharma. This was the first time when the Bhatts were working with a director who had not been trained in their production company and Anurag was therefore the last person to be signed for the project and was then duly introduced to the cast and crew. Later, Anurag got to hear how Mahesh had been recommending and pushing his name for the past year and a half. 'After a nine-day schedule, Mahesh Bhatt checked the edits of *Saaya* to ascertain the quality of my work, and thereafter never came on the sets again and even went ahead and signed me for their next film,' shares Anurag.

As per the Mumbai film industry practice, on completion, the trials for *Saaya* began on a Monday and went on till Thursday. As was expected, Anurag was afflicted with pre-release blues but was pleasantly surprised at the select audiences' reaction to his film – it had actually managed to scare and startle several people! Gradually, the nervousness of Monday turned into confidence by Thursday, a day prior to the movie's release on Friday. Meanwhile, one of India's premier English News channels, NDTV suggested that Anurag should do their "Meet the Audience" show that captured veiwers' response outside movie halls on the first day of a film's screening. Anurag agreed to host the show but when he saw people's reactions after the morning and noon shows in a theatre at Goregaon, he knew the film had bombed – portions where they were supposed to be horrified, there was uproarious laughter and worse, people began walking out of the movie hall midway, during the interval. It was now too late for Anurag to retract and committed that he was, he decided to shoot the elderly and women audiences coming out of the exit gate, presuming them to be less harsh in their criticism. And when the camera started rolling, some said, '*Hero achha hai* (The hero is good)'; one boy lunged towards the mike and said, '*Bakwas, paisa barbad* (Useless, money wasted). ' Anurag tried looking towards Tani for some comfort but she was also laughing along and did not oblige! Then suddenly one man came up and started saying positive things about the director of the film, almost like a professional critic – '*Acchi script hoti toh director achha kaam kar sakta tha*, etc. (If the script had been good, the director could have done a good job, etc).'A little later when the interviewing got over, the same man came back to Anurag, introduced himself as a struggling artist and asked, '*Aapka office kahan hai? Photo dena hai.* (Where is your office? I would like to leave my pictures with you).' Anurag was crestfallen and thought to himself, '*Yeh ek din baad aata toh!* (Only if he had said this 24 hours later!), I would have been happy for at least a day!' Meanwhile, the box office collection reports started pouring in from all over India and even though some initial trends seemed encouraging, the film was eventually declared a flop.

The next film the Bhatts wanted him to direct was titled *Zarooorat* but Anurag wanted to make *Murder* instead. 'I discussed the concept of *Murder* with Mukesh. Initially Mukesh wasn't convinced as he thought it was too alien a concept for Indian audiences. However, I was convinced and wrote and narrated the entire story to him. Later, he also saw merit in it and now there were two of us who wanted to make this film. Meanwhile, *Zaroorat's* first schedule was to commence soon and we had already shot a song sequence for it. Mukesh gave me a week's time to write the screenplay for *Murder* which I did and when Mahesh read it, he too was impressed with it. It was then decided that *Murder* would go on the floor first. However, *Zaroorat* was not shelved as HMV had partnered with Vishesh for the movie, and was hence merely postponed.

'I then began work on *Murder* at breakneck speed. Ashmit Patel and Emran's Hashmi's first movies had flopped at the box office and so they were easily available! We had spotted Mallika Sherawat—in an interview with Barkha Dutt on NDTV speaking boldly about the seventeen kisses in her first flop film, *Khwahish*—and she seemed a perfect fit for the role. So, everything worked out, *sabki dates easily mil gayi* (Everyone's dates were easily available) and that's how it all started. Each one of us needed a hit desperately. I was given complete freedom to make the movie my way and involved myself in the writing, music, and casting of the film.

'The shooting for *Murder* began with the song, *"Bheege honth tere"* which was sung by Kunal Ganjawala, and was wrapped overnight! You know it's strange, but during the shooting of a film, you can somehow feel it in your bones if it will eventually do well and I remember that feeling during the making of *Murder*. Of course, Tani's presence on the set helped immensely and particularly in getting the best out of Mallika,' shares Anurag about the making of his 2004 block-buster hit movie.

The year proved to be significant as it not only brought huge commercial success for Anurag, he also decided to sol-emnize his seven-year-long relationship with Tani and the two decided to get married during the making of *Murder*. Tani was no stranger to Anurag's family and in retrospect he feels grateful that she didn't insist on having a separate home and the Basus continue to live as a joint family till today.

Murder had a good run at the box office and proved to be a game changer for Vishesh Films which had been pilloried for a string of flops in the recent past. Soon thereafter, in 2006 Anurag followed it up with yet another successful film, *Gangster* which catapulted him and his discovery, Kangana Ranaut's career to staggering heights.

It was now time for Anurag to fulfill his commitment of completing *Zaroorat* (which was now renamed as *Tumsa Nahin Dekha*), but that was not to be. *'Woh film meri kismet mein hee nahin thi* (That film wasn't in my destiny),' he says. The reason: he was diagnosed with cancer. Just a few days before the casting of *Tumsa Nahin Dekha* was to commence, Anurag had started feeling unusually low and as a result, un-derwent some medical tests. He recalls how after the medical reports were obtained, he saw his parents' fallen faces and knew that something drastic had happened to him. He won-dered if it was HIV or cancer, and then the doctor told him the much dreaded truth, it was leukemia.

During the initial stages of cancer, he often felt "normal" but soon thereafter, the cancer cells multiplied at a rapid pace leading to profuse bleeding and raw blisters in his mouth. If the situation tried Anurag and Tani's perseverance the hardest, it was made worse after Tani discovered that she was pregnant and had to keep it a secret from her husband who was battling for his life. 'I was barely conscious to realize anything. Tani went through hell those days managing her pregnancy and my near-fatal condition, all by herself. My father could not bear to come inside my room. I looked ugly with a swollen face; people used to be shocked to see me. I remember once Mahesh Bhatt and Anupam Kher came to meet me at the hospital and Mahesh's hand shook uncontrollably when he touched my head and I could sense something serious had happened to me. I was sinking.

'One of my cousins then suggested that I should see Dr Sripad Banawali at the Tata Memorial Hospital. At this juncture, being part of the film industry proved to be a great advantage and on the late Sunil Dutt sahab's recommendation, I procured a bed in the hospital. I was immediately shifted from Lilavati to Tata and the drive during the transfer was by far the longest and most difficult of my life with recurrent traffic jams and my severe inability to breath; I later used that scene in my film, *Life in a Metro*. I was on ventilator support for the next eighteen days, hanging between life and death. My family went through hell. My father, who was fit till then, developed diabetes, blood pressure, etc. Instead of me taking care of Tani during her pregnancy, she was the one who was running around! But I was lucky to have found the right doctor and was subsequently given the Cancer Survivor of the Year award. Honestly, it's all thanks to my doctor.'

Anurag's one-and-a-half year long struggle with cancer emptied his bank account and to make matters worse, when he went out looking for work, no one was willing to bet on him. 'I don't blame them. Anyone would have done that. But the Bhatts stood by me and that's why till today, I am very close to them,' he acknowledges.

Meanwhile, Mukesh Bhatt waited for Anurag to recover completely before he could assign him the next film, but Anurag was a man in a hurry. 'I needed money to pay for my treatment. So I started approaching my friends in television and as soon I got an assignment, I started going to the sets with an oxygen mask, etc. When Mukesh heard about this, he called me. I had in the meanwhile written the story of *Life in a Metro* and narrated it to him. But he didn't want to make this film. The Bhatts are associated with a particular genre of films and they didn't want to try anything different. But Ronnie Screwvala, CEO of UTV Group, had liked *Gangster,* and when he heard the story of *Life in a Metro*, he came on board as a producer.'

Continues Anurag, 'After Metro, *Kites* happened with Filmkraft Productions of Rakesh Roshan. That film still flummoxes me. It was one of the biggest releases and yet didn't do well due to cost overruns and other such issues. I didn't want to apportion blame for its failure and accepted that the story didn't come from my heart and I therefore couldn't do justice to it. *Kites* was an urbane film, very distant from my small town sensibilities. It was clearly not my story and I decided that in the future I will only do my kind of stories.'

Meanwhile, during one of the screenings of *Life in a Metro*, Anurag was sitting outside a studio and was struck by the fact that he could understand the entire film by just listening to its audio. Since that moment, an idea which took root in his head and stayed for many years was of making a visually powerful film which would tell the story with more pictures than sound.

Later, during the shooting of *Kites*, he visited a home for children with special needs run by an NGO and met Murtaza and Razia who were autistic. One day, he saw that Razia was extremely upset with the world at large, and nobody could handle her except Murtaza who was also the caretaker of that home. The incident moved Anurag to such an extent that he decided to develop it further and the result was *Barfi*. When the inmates of the home went for *Barfi's* screening,

Farzana, their teacher called Anurag from outside the theatre and told him how they instantly recognized their Razia and Murtaza in Priyanka and Ranbir. 'This gesture was the biggest award for Tani and I, not the several that the film eventually bagged. I am aware that before *Barfi*, there have been several films on differently abled people, but I am told and would like to believe that *Barfi* portrayed them sensitively and succeeded in evoking emotions like none other. ' For the last couple of years, Anurag has taken to maintaining a record about people, incidents etc., that touch his heart and hopes that all of it will feature in his films, some day.

Anurag considers his father, who passed away in 2008, to be the strongest influence in his life. His mother, Deepshika who was once involved in the dubbing department with her son, now runs a boutique. Anurag believes that the rights and wrongs in his life are the rights and wrongs of his parents; life is a continuation of what they handed over to him and just as in screen writing there is a clichéd line, *"Film ka first half agar achha ho, toh second half bhi achha hota hai* (If the first half of a film is good, then the second half is bound to be good)"—he believes that's true for his life as well.

In the speed and gallop of life, and particularly after his illness, Anurag's priorities underwent a complete transformation. His family has become the key focus for him especially his daughters, Ishana and Ahana who are in junior school.

At Anurag's suggestion, we continue the rest of our discussion during the drive from Malad to Lokhandwala where his next meeting is scheduled. A short distance away, a huge poster of *Kai Po Che* peers at us. I want to know if he would also consider making films with newcomers in the future?

He responds quickly and says that though he wants to cast newcomers, *'Par film banane ke liye paise chahiye* (You need money to make films). The producers invest more money if a film has big stars. I wish I could give chances to more talent as besides the lead actors, we also need artists for various other roles. It's sad that we don't have a single platform from where we can source talented artists. Our own guild or the artists' union should have a site whereby if anyone wants a role, say a forty-year-old person from a certain area of the country, we can look at casting him while sitting here in Mumbai, just as it is done abroad.'

How did he feel when *Barfi* failed to make the cut at the 85th Academy Awards? I pose my next question.

'If I say that in India we make a big brouhaha about the Oscars when countries like Korea, China, Japan, etc don't attach so much importance to it, it may sound like a case of "sour grapes"! The Oscars are a Hollywood-led award function. Due to the huge media spends by the Academy Awards, we have been conditioned to believe that they are the best, whereas that's not true! I am as happy with recognition at Busan, Taipei or Okinawa film festivals or *Barfi* receiving accolades at WIPO in UN. Those were big achievements for the film, no less than the Oscar, which the media refuses to cover.'

What are his views about some of the films that form part of the "100 crore club", that many think are trash?

'No film is trash! And a film that makes 100 crores is certainly not, for the fact that it has entertained people and liked by a certain class of people. *Aapko nahin acchi lagti, aap mat dekhiye* (If you don't like it, don't watch it).'

Has there been any particular moment that has been creatively most satisfying for you, I ask?

'If I were to remember one such moment, it would mean that I am not creating anything new. Creativity is like a drug, it's addictive and you have to be constantly creating something new to feel good.'

Your movies usually have good music, what's your style of working to get the music right?

'Pritam Chakraborty and I work very closely. Our taste in music is very similar. I am the quintessential Jack of all trades and master of none, *jo film industry mein kaam aata hai* (which works in the film industry), not anywhere else. I can't play any instruments or sing but I have a good ear for music. It's important to communicate to your music director what's in your head in order to enable him to create the right sounds. So we have these long jamming sessions and then emerges the right music. Sometimes I am scared of losing that judgement. I normally like to go with what is needed in the film and not to remain under pressure to deliver a hit. That's the criteria I apply to the entire filmmaking process too. The criteria is not that *yeh film chalegi ki nahin* (whether this film will work or not), the criteria is whether it will make me happy. Technically, making a film without being in love with it is unworkable. You have to work on the set every day. How can you do that if you are not in love with it or if you start feeling *pack up kab hoga* (when will we pack up for the day)? My crew members and I must enjoy every day of the shoot,' are his conclusive remarks.

Anurag Basu's next film is also being produced by UTV. What fragrance of his small town, unpretentious sensibilities will he translate on the screen this time; will it match up to *Barfi's* stupendous success or be "sweeter"? Only time will tell… what's however certain is that as a brilliant director and a finer human being, he has been an asset for the film industry and shall continue to add tremendous value to it.

'Creativity is addictive like a drug… You have to be constantly creating something new to feel good.'

THE PERFECTIONIST
ASHUTOSH GOWARIKER

The first time I called Ashutosh to set up a meeting, he was away in Doha representing India as member of the jury for the Tribeca Film Festival. Soon thereafter, he was away to receive honours for his 2008 magnum opus, *Jodhaa Akbar* at the Marrakech International Film Festival. On his return from Morocco, I meet him at his office located on 15th road, Khar West on the 4th floor of a plush building called, Fortune Classic.

The large and classy office, I learn is the "Director's office" and there is another a few yards away on 14th road which is used for production. Ashutosh tells me later that he is a quintessential Bandra boy and lives in the vicinity, on 16th road, in the same building where he was born and neighbours with yesteryear actress, Kumkum!

I see Ashutosh entering through a different entrance of the room looking stately and dignified even though casually dressed in jeans and a shirt. Perhaps the dignity and composure with which he conducts himself has to do with his father having been part of the Maharashtra police force for long years. Ashutosh's mother was a home maker and brought up Ashutosh and his younger sister, Aslesha, while pursuing classical music at home. The Gowariker couple was extremely fond of the arts—cinema, theatre, and music—and took their young children along for several such performances. Additionally, very early on, even while Ashutosh was in junior school, his parents introduced him to Marathi literature and by the time he turned ten, he had already read two volumes on Shivaji by the eminent Marathi historian, B M Purandare. 'All that learning remained in my subconscious. Today when I look back, I use all those influences in my movies. Perhaps the indirect film atmosphere of my neighbourhood also left an influence on me. Although as a child I never harboured ambitions that *ek din bada hokar main actor banoonga* (I shall become an actor when I grow up), now when I look back, I think it did affect me in some ways,' he reflects.

On completing his class ten from St Theresa High School, close home at Bandra West, Ashutosh joined Mithibai College in Juhu and discovered that he was drawn to Architecture. 'But my labour at academics did not match my ambition. With a 52% score in class twelve, Architecture was a closed chapter,' he discloses with a wry smile. The next three years of college were spent doing a regular B.Sc. course and Ashutosh decided to flow with the tide.

Amongst several others, Mithibai College in Mumbai enjoys a great reputation for encouraging the performing arts, with a special focus on dramatics. During the first two months of college, Ashutosh discovered that multiple auditions were being held in Mithibai for roles in Marathi, Gujarati, English and Hindi plays, as well as talent hunts in folk dances, singing, etc. He went for every audition and was pleasantly surprised because not only was he selected, this was the first time when he had even attempted something like this! 'I went for these auditions more as a bystander with a group of students, but when I got selected, I felt that I did something right. Even though I bagged small roles, those moments on stage were very significant for me. I decided that if the theatre director had so much faith in me, I must repay him.'

His first director, Ashok Pandit, and the second, Naushil Mehta—both later went on to make a name for themselves—were at the time trying to get a break into the theatre scene in Mumbai. Ashutosh put in his best to impress them and even participated in folk dance competitions, which he had never done before. There was of course yet another pleasant reason for his enthusiasm—Sunita, who was one of his partners in a folk dance performance! 'We have been dancing ever since,' Ashutosh comments lightheartedly about his wife. Sunita was pursuing Humanities and was two years junior to him. She stayed close by at Pali Hill in Bandra and also had a distant connection with the world of films as Deb Mukherji (brother of Joy and Shomu Mukherji and father of director, Ayan Mukherji) happened to be her stepfather.

In time, one of the plays Ashutosh participated in became a huge success. One day, the renowned filmmaker, Ketan Mehta who was casting for his next film came to see the play and was greatly impressed with what he saw unfold on stage and decided to cast young Ashutosh in his forthcoming film titled, *Holi* in a lead role alongwith Aamir Khan, Amol Gupte, Raj Zutshi and Neeraj Vora. Soon thereafter, things began to fall in place and not only did Ashutosh's family support him fully, even his college granted him exemption from lectures and terminals.

Although *Holi* did not fit the definition of mainstream cinema, it won a lot of critical acclaim after it was selected by the International Film Festival of India (IFFI) for the panorama section that year. However, for Ashutosh, *Holi* became a passport to the film industry and the source of his first ever income, which was all of 7,500 bucks! He was still finishing his second year of college and having already acted in a film in a lead role gave him and his family a great sense of achievement. But with no roots in the film business, he still didn't take cinema seriously.

'*Holi* was seen by a whole lot of people including Bhatt sahab who later cast me in *Naam*. Amol Palekarji also cast me in a television series called *Kachchi Dhoop*. I met people and got more work. And finally, I had to take the important decision of choosing acting as a fulltime profession. I had a deep realization that acting had helped me grow and seemed a powerful medium in engaging with the audiences. I was all of twenty-one and enjoying the process. After much mulling over, I decided to go ahead with the opportunity. All these developments seemed quite sudden and surprising to Sunita too with whom I was in a steady relationship by now. She graduated a year after me, flew with Air India for a while, did some modelling assignments and took in her own experiences. We got married when I was twenty-four,' shares Ashutosh.

In a way, the process of acting readied him for a career in direction and he elaborates how, 'When one watches a film as an audience, it is consumed as a whole and one doesn't really bifurcate the process. But as an actor on the set, I could see the compartmentalization – how the sound recordist was as important as the Director of Photography (DOP), how costume design and art were important in a film, why colours could not clash, how there were different kinds of actors, some who were technically so savvy that they understood the camera and knew how much to perform in a close or a wide shot and so on and so forth. I was very alert to the process on the set,' he shares about his early learnings.

After five to six years as an actor, Ashutosh realized that he was getting into a direction mode and felt a compelling desire to tell stories, something he had immensely enjoyed since childhood. There used to be a competition amongst his neighbourhood kids – who amongst them would get to see the "first day, first show" of a film and narrate the story to the rest? Everybody wished Ashutosh would as he had a special talent of spicing it up with realtime action sequences, sound effects and drama! Further, after having spent a few years in the industry albeit as an actor, Ashutosh realized that a director's role was akin to a conductor's in an opera who may not know how to play the trombone, drum or the harp but is still able to orchestrate a symphony. Similarly, he observed that a director may not be aware of every technical detail in filmmaking, but with the help of an efficient team, still succeed in making a good film. This fascination kept nudging him towards direction.

Moreover, three of his contemporaries strongly believed that he had the talent to direct a film. First was Aamir Khan with whom he had acted in his debut film, the second, Deepak Tijori who studied at Narsee Monjee college and was his rival in college competitions and the third, Shah Rukh Khan with whom he had co-starred in films like *Kabhi Haan Kabhi Naa (KHKN)* and *Chamatkaar* and in the TV series, *Circus*. Apart from the professional association, Ashutosh would meet them socially or sometimes to play a game of cricket or tennis, etc.

Very soon his first opportunity in direction came through Deepak Tijori who was being cast by producers, Viral Shah and Mr. Rahim in *Pehla Nasha*. Deepak recommended Ashutosh for his debut film. In fact before *Pehla Nasha*, Ashutosh was supposed to make *Baazi* with Aamir Khan but since the actor's dates didn't materialize, he went ahead with *Pehla Nasha* which was eventually released as his first film.

'The producers of both the films (Salim Akhtar for *Baazi*) did not know me but they trusted the actors who were recommending me. So it became simpler for me to get a break as a director, as I didn't have to convince Messers Money Bags! At times, I used to wonder at the immense faith reposed by Aamir and Deepak in someone like me who had no prior experience. And frankly, that doesn't cease to amaze me till date,' confesses Ashutosh.

As a debutant director, were you offered a decent remuneration? How was your first contract structured, was it some sort of a partnership, I want him to share the details.

'There was no fee. I was willing to bring home-cooked food to the set. So thankfully, I didn't have to pay the guys to give me a break!' he says. We break at this point to meet again and there's more of Ashutosh's light-hearted humour that awaits me!

Prior to our second meeting, I receive a mail from him saying that we could meet on 1 April. Before this, a couple of last minute cancellations had already taken place due to some unavoidable engagements at his end. Promptly, yet another mail followed from him saying, 'This time it's final, don't let the date bother you!' And that's when it struck me to relook at the date!

We meet at a new venue – at his aesthetically-done production office on the ground floor of Prabhat building on 14th road. Continuing from our earlier discussion regarding remuneration, he talks about the unspoken rule in the industry, which is if a film makes money, then the director also makes money. 'Usually only successful directors get into partnerships. It's only when you have brand equity that you might be offered a partnership', he says.

Eventually, his first two films proved to be big setbacks for him as they didn't have the kind of box office success he had expected. 'Initially I reacted by putting the blame on the audience saying that they had failed to understand my vision. However, as the dust settled, I understood that the problem was with me. The kind of story I had selected, the screenplay, the narrative I'd employed, it was as if I was too eager to please the audience. But by the time I realized this, it was already too late. I was out of work. My directorial shop was shut. But thanks to my acting background, I was offered an acting assignment to play the role of a cop in the television series, *CID*. I did a few more television serials and took up advertising assignments as well.'

Was it unnerving to face failure so early? How did you cope with the uncertainty in the industry? I want him to share his insights.

He replies, 'The minute you become part of the film business, you contend with the fact that it's like quicksand. You might have an extremely good two-year period followed by a four-year lean period. I think it requires a lot of perseverance and good fortune to hang in here. There are scores of talented people who arrive in Mumbai and even more who leave every day as they can't sustain the pressures. It's all a part of showbiz. But thankfully I survived because I continued acting and was rooted in Mumbai.'

By then Ashutosh had decided that if he ever returned to direction, it would only be with a convincing script. Therefore, alongside his acting assignments, he began writing the story for his next film (which took almost three years to complete), which would not only prove to be a blockbuster hit but win unprecedented international acclaim; none other than the glorious, *Lagaan*.

As is well known, *Lagaan's* nomination for the Academy Awards in 2002 was a watershed moment for the Indian film industry—after *Mother India* (1957) and *Salaam Bombay* (1988), it was the third Hindi-language film to be nominated in the Best Foreign Language Film category! Recalling those halcyon days, Ashutosh shares, 'It was amazing to be present amongst so many greats from all over the world, not just Hollywood but also from European cinema, the Far East and other countries. It was great to see such energy and vibrancy for cinema and the immense respect for directors and actors. Just the celebration of cinema was something unforgettable. There are so many awards and festivals but the Oscar is the only one that beats even the Cesar which is the French film award function. Although cinema first took root in Paris, the Academy Awards have taken over and become more central, with an unparalleled reach. If you win an Oscar, your film gets a second lease of life by way of satellite, DVDs, theatricals and such rights. Having the tag of an Oscar win makes it go global which no other award guarantees. Those are the amazing benefits of being an Academy Award nominee and winner.'

Lagaan finally lost the Academy Award to the Bosnian film, *No Man's Land.* The country was of course hugely disappointed. How did he view this failure, I ask him?

'When we send a film to the Oscars, the pressure exerted by the media on winning is unrealistic. Why should that kind of hype and pressure be built? Do you know which are the other fifty-two films from other countries? Do you have any idea that there are at least five films out of those fifty-two that have won in the Venice, Cannes or Korean film festivals; they have been blazing victories before entering the Oscars? So till you don't know your opponent, why would you feel so strongly about your own entry—just because you liked it; that's not enough. It's like saying that your school-going child will top the class. How do you know? You don't know how the other kids are faring! So I strongly feel that we first need to select our most distinctive film, make sure that it impacts the judges and focus on the entire process because *orchestrating* a win at the Oscars is as important as producing a good film. It takes preparation, you have to swing views and make people think in a different way. I think we don't do enough towards creating an adequate buzz for our films. It's true that ultimately the film speaks for itself but it needs support from the media, PR, marketing and promotion to make it globally relevant.'

I probe further. Do you think that a film, made exclusively with the Oscars in mind stands a good chance of winning?

Ashutosh has a clear view on this, 'I don't think you should choose a story or make a film to win an Oscar. A filmmaker should make a film because he wants to make it.'

Our filmmakers seem to be more interested in being part of the "100 crore club" than the haloed club of Academy Award winners? I prompt him to comment on this.

'You cannot put the entire film industry in one basket. Yes, there is one section which believes in making commercially successful films and for them the Oscar is not so important. However, there is also another section which believes that their films should have a creative appeal and for them the Oscars are like the Olympics, the ultimate goal. I think all approaches co-exist. Even in Hollywood, when an Arnold Schwarzenegger makes a film, he doesn't think that he is going to win an Oscar for it! He focuses on the box office. Martin Scorsese on the other hand, focuses on the Academy Awards. So different points of view will always exist, to each his own. Ultimately the story that you select for a film will have its own destiny and one has to accept that.'

Does being on the world stage open up opportunities for a director like him to make films with cross border associations, I fire the next salvo.

'Yes it does,' he explains, 'you can do such projects but you have to relocate, give up everything and embrace Hollywood or London. Both, *Life of Pi* and *Slumdog Millionaire* were Indian themes, but made by foreigners—Danny Boyle and Ang Lee respectively. It's directed by them, produced out of Hollywood, the money is from the overseas. You cannot call them *Indian* films. If you want to create a global impact, you have to go through Hollywood and make a film in English. Recently, Reliance made inroads into Hollywood and co-produced *Lincoln* and *Warhorse*. That's the way to collaborate.

As for me, I see myself operating pretty much in the space of Hindi films. If there is a good offer, I don't mind going out and relocating for some time. But I shall always return.'

As the experience with the elite Academy Awards happens to be Ashutosh's sole privilege amongst contemporary filmmakers, it was natural for me to discuss its various aspects with him. Shifting focus to the next film after *Lagaan*, I ask him why he opted for a low budget film like *Swades* after the stupendous success of *Lagaan*. Afterall, producers would have opened up their coffers to do magnum opus projects with him?

Spelling out his fundamental approach to filmmaking, Ashutosh says, 'I just wanted to focus on my next work. For me the script was most important, not the monies. I wanted to reset everything to zero and begin work. The glory of *Lagaan* was for *Lagaan*. Of course it gave me a positioning and I had the freedom to make my next film my way. I used it for *Swades*,' he explains.

By no stretch was *Swades* a box office smash but the huge critical acclaim it received, gave Ashutosh yet another opportunity to exercise his creative freedom and this time with a film which was infinitely bigger in scale. It was the magnum opus historical-drama, *Jodhaa Akbar* set in sixteenth century India which amongst several other things, mainly focused on the theme of religious tolerance relevant to contemporary times.

All your films, except *What's Your Raashee,* have a message. Does this aspect form the core of your filmmaking? I want him to share his approach.

'Fundamentally cinema, I feel must entertain but I also feel very strongly that it should have a message. It can either be a moral or social message or something that brings about a change in the viewer. If you make a comedy, you don't have to get into that space but in drama or any other genre, which has a scope for a message, you must not only entertain but also share your message. I like to keep the theme of my films very simple; they might seem individualistic but should have a universal appeal. When I select a story, my entire focus is in approaching it in a manner that the intended message comes across undiluted. So it may be a group of people coming together to fight a common enemy, which is *Lagaan* or a person who is rediscovering his roots, how his thinking undergoes change, and how he struggles to initiate a change with or without support—that became the basis for *Swades*. Religious tolerance became the theme for *Jodhaa Akbar*. These themes get embedded within the story. The other critical factor is the method and setting one adopts to make the theme impact the audiences. For me, cricket became a very important vehicle for *Lagaan*. When it came to *Jodhaa Akbar*, I could have told a story about a Muslim family in Mumbai and a Hindu family in Gwalior and how they respect each other's religion. But I thought of adding splendour and grandeur and that's how *Jodhaa Akbar* happened.'

All your movies have been made with big stars, why don't you launch new actors?

He reasons, 'In my case, the story is an experiment in itself and I would rather not experiment with my casting! In my film, if I have villagers playing cricket, it's such an absurd idea that you need an Aamir to make it work; for a historical drama like *Jodhaa Akbar*, you need Aishwarya Rai Bachchan and Hrithik Roshan to capture the splendour; or a Shah Rukh Khan to play Mohan Bhargava for *Swades* to seem plausible! If I have a small film, say a contemporary theme or a thriller, then maybe I won't need a star and may launch a new face. For other kind of films, a star ensures a wider reach. When I want to tell a story with a message, I want it to reach the maximum number of people and a star makes that possible. That said, I don't work with fixed notions; star or no star, the option remains open, to be decided film by film.'

Several directors are able to churn out movies at a fast pace. They are involved in the direction and production of multiple movies simultaneously. The last movie that was released under your banner was *Khelein Hum Jee Jaan Se*, in 2010. Have you ever considered approaching direction and production together and releasing films at a faster pace?

Explains Ashutosh, 'There's no linear approach to this and everyone needs to figure out how much one can do and handle. If I am involved in a script, it absorbs me completely. I don't like to multitask. I can perhaps work on three scripts at the same time, but I definitely can't shoot three movies simultaneously! Then there are others who are able to make their movie and produce for others. They possibly have a wider range of administrative skills. It's like actors, someone does one film a year and there are others who act in four. Ideally, I would like to do one film a year. But usually my scripts need preparation for a year or more. Getting the script right is an all-consuming process for me; they are detailed and 80% of direction happens at that stage itself. Even for the music in my films, I like to have the detailed setting and emotion on paper. I am of the opinion that lyrics are nothing more than dialogues converted into rhyme and with the help of a music composer, it becomes a song and enhances the scene through emotions—joy, sadness etc. In case of period films, the preparation before shooting is even more tedious as there are additional departments to be handled like the costumes, props, language and syntax for dialogues, etc. I like to do the R&D for a film myself, simply because it becomes a valuable aid for me when I am finally directing the film. For me the process of filmmaking is sacrosanct. I should be enriched at the end of it.'

I discover that Ashutosh is an ardent supporter of film education. His elder son, Konark recently completed a four-year undergraduate course in film production from Emerson College, Boston and the younger one, Vishwang is likely to follow suit after finishing senior school from the Dhirubhai Ambani International School. Ashutosh reveals that before making *Pehla Nasha,* he had completed a forty-five day course in film appreciation from the Film and Television Institute of India or FTII, so desperate was he to acquire some technical knowledge before plunging into the role of a director. 'Those were life changing days for me. I was eager to grasp the most in that limited time. I would devote 18-19 hours per day as I knew that this was the only chance I had. Though I wish I had done a two or a four-year course... I sincerely feel that those who have the opportunity and funds should educate themselves before joining the industry. They should study all schools of acting, watch films known for best performances, read as much literature as possible. The more you know, the easier it becomes to apply yourself to the craft. The more you know about technique and different forms of cinema, the easier it becomes to assimilate, create and express yourself through your films.'

In more ways than one, Ashutosh Gowariker broke the mould when he stepped out from his family to embrace cinema and also put a film like *Lagaan* on the world map. As a natural progression, I reckon the father-son duo of Ashutosh and Konark are going to make a formidable team, combining a wealth of experience and mastery over latest technique, while redefining Indian cinema! What films will roll out under the banner of AGPPL (Ashutosh Gowariker Productions Private Limited) is certainly something that is going to be observed closely in the coming years!

... '*Orchestrating* a win at the Oscars is as important as producing a good film. It takes preparation, you have to swing views and make people think in a different way. I think we don't do enough towards creating an adequate buzz for our films.'

"Jeena yahan marna yahan, iske siwa jaana ka-han," seems as if the Raj Kapoor song from the 1970 film, *Mera Naam Joker,* was specifically written for film families: the Khans (not just Aamir, Salman or Shah Rukh, but also Farah!), the Roshans, the Kapoors, the Chopras, the Bhatts et al. Born to filmmaker Kamran Khan and Menka Irani (youngest sister of Daisy and Honey Irani), Farah, in more ways than one, was destined to become a Bollywood director. Her personal life hasn't been any less *filmy* than some of the intensely melodramatic movies that Bollywood is known for. Much in the same vein and punctuated with dramatic highs and lows, hers is a "riches to rags to riches" story spanning over forty years.

I meet Farah at her 34th floor penthouse at Oberoi Heights in Lokhandwala. The *"filmy* touch" is evident right from the driveway that leads to the imposing and well decorated lobby of the building, guarded by a battery of security men keenly watching the multiple computer screens and manning an efficient communication system. I am politely escorted by one of them, via the elevator meant for guests, to her beautiful apartment. A long ledge outside the main door carries artistic plaques that announce the names of the residents—not only Farah and Shishir's but their much famous triplets, Anya, Diva and Czar's too!

The door opens into a gigantic hall, divided into the living room, dining space and a lounge that overlooks a creek through the glass wall. The entire place has a very open and relaxed feel about it. Dressed in a baby pink outfit, Farah is looking her best– elated with the recent success of her *Jumping Jhapak* IPL TVC and perhaps more importantly, because of the inner calm and happiness that she has found with Shishir and their three little children.

Farah's father, Kamran was a Bollywood actor in the late Fifties-early Sixties when he met Menka Irani. Even though Menka was twenty years younger, she fell in love with him and eloped to marry him. Farah was their first child and five years later her brother, Sajid was born.

Initially, much like other Bollywood kids, Farah and Sajid had a comfortable childhood, but all that changed when one day, on an impulse their father, Kamran suddenly decided to give up acting and turned to film production and direction. Unfortunately, his initiatives misfired at the box office and from that moment onwards, a downward spiral began for the Khan family. The resultant financial difficulties coupled with Kamran's infidelity put a strain on his marriage with Menka which finally ended in a divorce when Farah was in class eight. Menka moved out to a paying guest accommodation in Bandra and took up work as a housekeeping staff in one of the hotels to support herself while Farah and Sajid continued to live with their father and grandmother in a rented flat in Juhu. The unstable family environment had a huge impact on Farah. From being at the top of her class at St Theresa School in Bandra, her academic performance started slipping as she struggled to cope with the emotional trauma of her parents' separation, her father's increasing alcoholism and her family's critical financial situation.

One day, while little Farah was caring for her father, Kamran died a broken man, leaving the family to fend for itself, despite a clutch of rich relatives and fair weather friends. With Kamran's passing, Menka moved back to the Juhu flat with her children.

Meanwhile life moved on and after school, Farah chose to study Sociology at St Xavier's College, Mumbai where her passion for dancing finally took root. Even as a child, Farah was famous for her dancing skills and would often entertain her family and friends with her ebullient performances. Those were the mid-Eighties when cover versions of pop groups and artists like Boney-M and Michael Jackson were a rage amongst college students and Farah obsessed with MJ, would practice for hours to dance like him. Soon thereafter, Farah decided to make a living out of her passion and formed a band with four of her boyfriends called, Sphinx. The group was one of its kind at the time and soon became a rage in the western pop and rock music scene in Mumbai. The band was, as they say, on a roll and managed to win every competition and after one such win, was even invited to a dance championship in London.

On the one hand, if dancing became the fulcrum of Farah's life and earned her both money and recognition, it also became the sole reason for her dropping out of college due to poor attendance. There was more trouble in store for young Farah in the shape of a love relationship which her mother, Menka strongly disapproved. In order to get her mind off the boy, Menka arranged for Farah to go to Bangalore and work as an assistant director with the late Shankar Nag on his iconic television serial, *Malgudi Days*, broadcast on Doordarshan in the mid-Eighties. This was Farah's first introduction to the world of cinema. However, it would take her a good seventeen years to make her debut as a director and only after spending an entire decade and a half as a well known choreographer!

Soon after her return from Bangalore, the beginner's luck was waiting to shine on her yet again and made its way with the debut film of Mansoor Khan, *Jo Jeeta Wohi Sikander* in 1992. After winding up *Malgudi Days*, Farah was soon looking for work and was introduced to Mansoor Khan by one of her musician friends. Mansoor hired her as an assistant director for the film which was being choreographed by none other than the supremely talented Saroj Khan who was virtually "the master" of choreography at the time.

On one of those days while Saroj Khan was away for another shoot, Mansoor asked Farah to choreograph the song, *"Pehla nasha, pehla khumar"*. Farah made best use of the given opportunity to showcase her talent and the rest as we know is history. The song became a chartbuster. Farah received rave reviews for her choreography and ended up bagging her next full fledged choreography assignment with Kundan Shah for his 1994 movie, *Kabhi Haan Kabhi Naa (KHKN)* and most importantly, met Shah Rukh Khan for the first time on the sets of *KHKN*.

Exactly ten years after becoming friends, the duo would deliver their first super hit film as a director and producer respectively—*Main Hoon Naa (MHN)* in 2004 – the first movie to be written and directed by Farah Khan and the first to be produced by Shah Rukh Khan's company, Red Chillies Entertainment! Farah and Shah Rukh collaborated yet again for *Om Shanti Om (OSO)* in 2007, which witnessed greater success and became the highest-grossing Hindi film of all times.

By now, Farah Khan had clearly established herself as a trailblazer—the first woman choreographer-turned-successful director. There were indeed a few choreographers before her who had attempted direction, but to no avail. As far as women directors are concerned, most of them preceding her like, Sai Paranjpe, Aparna Sen, etc made wonderful albeit small niche films and I am sure there were more who tried their hand at mainstream films, but it's hard to find any parallels to Farah's success.

Farah, quite like the multifaceted-flamboyant director Karan Johar, is visible all over the entertainment space, from judging reality talent shows to hosting a celebrity chat show *(Tere Mere Beech Mein)*, featuring in television commercials and has also additionally done something that Karan hasn't yet tried—making international pop stars Shakira and Kylie Minogue dance to Bollywood tunes and playing the lead in a 2012 film titled, *Shireen Farhad Ki Toh Nikal Padi*. However, what she loves most and always wanted to do is direction and that's where she is focused right now—her fourth movie, *Happy New Year (HNY)*, to be released in 2014 – which she hopes will revive her earlier success and wipe out the humiliation of *Tees Maar Khan (TMK)* in 2010, a failure which still rankles deep in her heart.

If direction is what she always wanted to do, why did it take her more than a decade and a half to direct her first film, *MHN*, I ask as I admire the view from the beautiful lounge area of her penthouse where we are in conversation.

Farah tells me that it was her success as a choreographer which delayed her directorial debut. 'I was doing well as a choreographer and kind of worked non stop on those assignments. In hindsight, I can say that maybe I made *MHN* a good 3-4 years late. I wanted to make it earlier but it was just that the *gaadi* (meaning, the vehicle of life) was racing so fast that it took me time to pull the breaks. It was difficult for me to say, "No, I will not do your song, not do your movie." And the years slipped by. I remember how during the last three years before I made *MHN*, I used to be extremely irritable and edgy seeing everyone around me making movies and it was as if only I wasn't able to make one. Luckily it happened and did well too,' she explains.

What exactly is it that worked in her favour and gave her the privilege of being the first choreographer-turned-director of successful commercial films?

'Yes, that's true; no choreographer had succeeded as a director before me. There was no dearth of people who dissuaded me and advised how I was doing well as a choreographer and if I turned to direction and failed, my *dukaan* or shop will be shut. However, I was determined and believed that first, choreography is not a *dukaan* and second, I had the conviction that people always quote the past; you can't be led by their views. You have to venture out and break new ground. What I think worked for me was my vast experience in the industry, respect from my colleagues and most importantly, access to Shah Rukh. There were several producers who wanted me to direct their movies as they could see that I delivered, was organized, and shot in a specific time frame and budget. But I was clear that I wanted to wait for Shah Rukh Khan and make my first movie only with him,' says Farah, pronouncing her unshakable faith in the superstar's talent and mass appeal.

Did she face any difficulties as a woman director, I am curious to know as we walk towards the "elevator for residents" that opens inside each apartment; in her case, in the portion adjacent to the "gigantic hall" that houses the kitchen and bedrooms. Farah has an appointment coming up at a studio in Khar Linking Road and we had decided before setting up our meeting to carry on the rest of the conversation during the drive.

As we go down the 34th floor, a couple of other residents join in from other floors and chat with Farah about the latest episode of the dance reality show, *Nach Baliye* on Star Plus which she had co-judged with Shilpa Shetty and Terence Lewis. So, what does it take to be a woman director? Do they face more difficulties than men in this industry, I put the question to her again, once her chauffeur-driven Mercedes starts moving and I have finished giving instructions to my driver to trail us.

Farah promptly answers my question and says unequivocally, 'It's as difficult for a woman as it is for a man. It's just so difficult to get a film made, to get a star for your film. The studios may like your script but will agree to finance the film only if you can get a star. If your film is a big budget film, then unless you get a star of Shah Rukh Khan's stature, you won't get big monies from any producer, however big a director you may be. For new directors and script writers, the single most critical challenge is that they don't have access to stars. And if it's a small budget film, there is always a risk that it may not release at all. I can't imagine any studio saying, hey! we loved your script and *we* will make it with a new star! Once this aspect is taken care of, other than managing your personal life, the challenges are as easy or as difficult for a woman as they are for a man. The Mumbai film industry does not discriminate. All they want is someone who can deliver,' says Farah sharing the modus operandi of the industry's gender neutral work environment.

Your next movie, *Happy New Year* is a multi-starrer. So did the problem of getting stars on board delay the movie inordinately? I probe.

'Yes. In today's scenario it's difficult to make a movie like this with the kind of money each star wants and the innumerable date issues involved with various actors. Sometimes when I watch old movies which used to have six or seven big stars, I think that this can't be ever repeated in today's Bollywood! In fact, it's going to get more and more difficult because the youngsters don't want to do even a two-hero movie. The last time you saw so many stars (forty-two) getting along famously was perhaps in *OSO*.'

Was there a fee involved to get them on board?

'No, it was completely because of goodwill – 75% Shah Rukh's and 25% mine,' she shares.

Would you ever make a small budget film, I pose my next question.

Farah affirms that such a plan is afoot. 'That's the reason Shirish and I have started Three's Company, Three's Casting and Three's Content. We want new directors to send their scripts to us and we'll make small budget movies with them. We have plans to start a movie with a new director who has graduated from the FTII. Shirish read his script and loved it. We are casting new people for this film,' reveals Farah.

I want her to share her experiences with actors in general and if she perceives any changes in their attitudes over the years?

'I think a lot of things have changed over the years, while a lot still remain the same. One of the positive trends these days is that actors only do one film at a time or maximum two and dedicatedly finish it in a period of 5-6 months barring a few who still choose to do ten movies at a time. In the past, actors would do multiple movies and each would take at least two years to make. That was in the 70s and 80s and perhaps continued till the 90s. Therefore, actors are comparatively far more disciplined now. They report on time and are aligned to the producer and director. Every filmmaker today wants to wrap up the film in time – the faster you finish, the more money you save as your office runs for lesser duration and your payables are accordingly curtailed. It's the basic rule of any business.

'However, there are other things which are still the same. I have been here for the past twenty years. I still see arrogance in actors or actresses after their first hit movie. They don't realize that it's a cycle. They don't bother to look around and learn from people who have walked the same path before them. Yet another new trend that I now see is a breed of young, twenty-something-old, women-managers accompanying actresses. Earlier, there used to be the quintessential "star mommies" who would chaperone their daughters but in restrospect, I feel they were better than these new-age managers who brainwash actresses with all kinds of nonsense. So in some ways, the context is the same but the people involved have changed.'

What according to you is required for actors to get a break in a lead role? Being a star-son or -daughter is seemingly a clear advantage, I state wanting Farah to share the dynamics of making it big as an actor.

She says candidly, 'When you launch a girl, you could as well introduce someone from a non-film background. But in the case of a hero, you are bound to think, *"Kaun se hero ka beta bada ho gaya hai?"*(Which yesteryear actor's son has grown up) or is he a brother of so-and-so? Later, during the marketing and publicity of a movie, this factor definitely makes it that much easier. The producers feel, *"Uske baap ke fans toh aayenge dekhne ko*!(At least his father's fans will come to watch the film!)" For a commercial film, if the heroine is beautiful, winner of a beauty contest, can dance and carry off all kinds of outfits, people will still give her a chance, thinking, *"Woh acting seekh legi* (She'll learn how to act)." I guess it's also easier for a girl because in several Hindi movies, heroines are not required to do much whereas to a large extent, a hero is expected to carry a film on his shoulders. Therefore, if you observe minutely, very few men from outside the industry have got a break. No doubt, there are some movies that get released every year with newcomers but the question is how long will these newcomers sustain? Every year, a new guy is talked about and is no sooner written off too. Those who stay around for long are very few. Finally, it's all about consistency.'

And what's the key to sustain in the industry?

She replies, 'Some of our heroes have been around for more than twenty years and are still on top. The key factor? Well, all of them are extremely disciplined, have consistently honed their talent and are well spoken, intelligent, ambitious and ruthless. Over the years they have of course managed to also build a loyal fan following. With the girls however, the career graph tends to be shorter, though it's becoming better than what it used to be some years ago. Also if a heroine is just a pretty face and does the regular drill of two songs and a love scene, she will probably not end up sustaining for long. But then there are several other examples who are exceptionally talented like, Kajol, Kareena, Sridevi and Madhuri and who have therefore been around for long.'

And what does it take for a director to sustain in the industry? How does one cope with failure? After the resounding success of your first two movies, *MHN* and *OSO*, your next film, *Tees Maar Khan*, bombed badly?

Farah affirms and says, 'Post *OSO* was indeed a good space to be in. I have seen both sides—when every five minutes there would be a call congratulating you; one felt so wanted. It truly felt good that the movie was loved so much. And the other that was after *TMK*'s failure which was undoubtedly the lowest phase of my life! I began viewing things in a philosophical manner and foremost, not to take things too seriously and try and maintain equanimity, not get too excited when there is incredible praise nor get depressed with severe criticism. Accept the fact that you didn't make a good movie. If *TMK* had done well, I would have ignored the critics but the movie didn't do as well as we thought it should have. That was clearly the lowest point of my career. And then, there is another way to look at it. I feel, it's very important to see the lows. Afterall there isn't a single person who hasn't had a low in his career, ranging from biggies like Steven Spielberg to James Cameron and Raj Kapoor. You have to learn to handle failure and know that it's not the end of everything. What I find more unnerving is a sudden realization some day that I can't make a movie any more! When you know that you are good at your work and it's the movie that hasn't worked for you, you are fine.

'After *TMK*'s debacle, I spent one and a half years on *HNY*'s script. I wanted to make sure that we don't repeat the blunders. We did *TMK* in a hurry and even after its failure, you shall be surprised to know that there were several producers who wanted to sign me, but I desisted. Sometimes you have to be just patient, and not do things in a panic mode, otherwise chances are you'll make a wrong decision,' come forth the words of wisdom from Farah.

She played the lead in *Shirin Farhad Ki Toh Nikal Padi*, has judged innumerable reality shows and also hosted one. Is there anything else that she wishes to do? I ask.

Farah happily shares her current state of mind and responds calmly, 'I am open to what comes my way but am not chasing anything. I have a very different life now with my kids and husband. I am attending play dates with school moms rather than Bollywood parties where everyone networks! I genuinely feel that I am in a secure place and don't need to make a movie every year. I am not in that rat race any more. I am happy doing a movie every three years and enjoying those years of movie making.'

Does she see her children taking to films in the future?

As someone deeply entrenched in the film industry, she has a very good assessment to offer—'I love being part of the movies and have done reasonably well. Shirish and I will continue to make movies. So I don't see my son becoming a doctor, though right now my son wants to become an astronaut and one of my daughters wants to be a forensic expert! I think people should do what they want to. I will never force my kids into doing something they are not happy doing. If they want to be artists or musicians, it's fine as long as they are happy in their lives. However, it's the recognition, the power that comes with films that draws people to it, including children who grow up in this environment. It's the insatiable hunger for fame, for being in the public eye and not so much about the money that makes people take to films. So my guess is that my children will eventually do something related to films.'

How much value do you place on education? Would you want your children to join the business after high school or you want them to go to college? I put my pet question to her wanting to gather filmmakers' diverse perspectives on education.

She is clear about the advantage that education brings and says emphatically, 'I stood out amongst my peers as I was the only choreographer who was a graduate. Education opens out the whole world and newer horizons for you. I used to read a lot, subscribe to the cinematographer's magazine to understand how the songs and scenes were shot, watch Hollywood movies, read about the making of these movies, all of which made me grow as an artist and have an edge over others. I also became better spoken and could connect with people. I believe I am still in that space because I learn each day and therefore am able to connect with the new generation. School and college are wonderful parts of life and if you have both talent and knowledge, it definitely takes you far,' she concludes as we get out of her car, after having chatted for nearly an hour.

The Farah Khan I met came across as woman who has her priorities worked out in life. Having mostly seen the lighter side of her persona, I was actually taken by surprise at her clarity of thought and tremendous abilities as an organizer, qualities most required in a successful director besides several others. I think her best years may still be ahead of her!

'The challenges are as easy or as difficult for a woman director as they are for a man. The Mumbai film industry does not discriminate. All they want is someone who can deliver.'

LIFE IS AN ADVENTURE

KABIR KHAN

If there was a "Tiger" on screen in the historic 2012 blockbuster film, *Ek Tha Tiger*, there was another behind the camera too. A love for hardy, treacherous war zones and penchant for politically sensitive issues are essentially what define director "Tiger" Kabir Khan's cinema.

Although Kabir's lineage can be traced back to an aristocratic family in Hyderabad, he is, for all practical purposes, a Delhi person—having studied at Modern School and Air Force School, later at Kirori Mal College where he did Economics (Hons) and finally, Jamia Millia where he pursued an MA in Mass Communications. His father was a renowned academician and headed the Political Science department at Osmania University followed by Jawaharlal Nehru University or JNU and was subsequently nominated for two consecutive terms to the Rajya Sabha in the Seventies.

I am glad that Kabir has been able to make some time from his extremely busy schedule on this rather chilly Mumbai evening in January 2014. The shooting for his next film, *Phantom* starring Saif Ali Khan and Katrina Kaif has been in full swing and the third schedule is to begin two days later in Kashmir. He keeps his promise and we meet at the producer, Nadiadwala Grandson Entertainment Pvt Ltd's swish office on the 17th floor of Lotus Grandeur in Andheri West. This part of Mumbai's skyline looks quite captivating at the twilight hour from the huge balcony which is preferred for a chat by us rather than the stylish cabin inside. Kabir exchanges a few notes with his friend and line producer, Rajan regarding issues related to bad weather pointed out by the advance team in Kashmir before our conversation can begin.

In retrospect, Kabir attributes his early influence of cinema exclusively to his mother who was a great film buff and remembers how he and his sister, Anusha would accompany her to watch almost every Amitabh Bachchan starrer back then. Besides, there also used to be weekly "special screenings" at the Vigyan Bhawan, Delhi, for Members of Parliament where they would watch the cinema of Truffaut, Godard and several others from new wave French and Italian cinema. 'At that age, I used to hate those films but as we were constantly exposed to them, we gradually developed a taste for good cinema,' says Kabir with a sly grin. Further, Shyam Benegal happened to be a good friend of the Khan family, having directed Kabir's mother in plays, and as a result, starting from his first film *Ankur*, Kabir watched all his subsequent films.

So while Kabir's early years were influenced by his mother's love for cinema and father's academic and political engagements, it was in college that he discovered his other loves, the foremost being trekking and mountaineering. He would often backpack with his friends and spend months camping in the Himalayas and Ladakh, which remain his favourite terrain in the world. It was during his trekking expeditions that he developed a love for photography and began documenting his travels.

Meanwhile, inspired by one of his uncles, who had joined the UN after a degree in Economics, Kabir planned his career on the same lines and more out of his passion for wanderlust! However by the end of three years in college, he decided against Economics and put his plans of extensive travel on hold! 'In fact I was a bit of a drifter. After ruling out Economics, I was thinking of doing Law like my grandfather who was a lawyer or maybe pursue a Management degree. But I was still searching, trying to find my space,' he says, typically voicing the uncertainties of a young adult in college. It was around this time when his sister, Anusha was getting ready to apply to Jamia Millia. Kabir casually asked her to get him a form also and as luck would have it, this fluke attempt eventually led him to qualify along with Anusha and both landed in the same batch of the reputed Mass Communication course at the institute.

'That's how I drifted into Jamia. But once I was there, I knew I had found my calling and since then enjoyed it thoroughly. Even today, I never feel as if I have *worked* for a single day of my life,' he affirms. His love for the course resulted in his topping his batch, even though he admits that he was neither the industrious type nor someone who excelled in academics!

Kabir's first project after graduating from Jamia was a four-series documentary with the renowned journalist and close family friend, Saeed Naqvi, who was then producing a news feature for Doordarshan. Kabir admired Naqvi for his sharp political analyses and quick wit and remembers often being told by him, '*Train ho jao, aur phir karna kaam mere saath tv mein* (First get some training and you can then work with me in television).'

Thus began Kabir's tryst with high adventure and he travelled to the Central Asian Republics of Uzbekistan, Turkmenistan, Tajikistan and Kyrgyzstan for his four-series documentary and to several other destinations all over the world for later projects with Saeed. Besides a dream come true, and one of the most fulfilling ones with fifty-odd destinations thrown in, the experience with Naqvi broadened Kabir's worldview and shaped his perspective. He began to minutely observe how there was always a hidden story behind big stories. 'If you analyze my films in the mainstream space, there is something which comes from Saeed's line of thought that how there's essentially a huge gap between what is reported and what is actually there at ground level. My stories lie in that gap. These are stories that are never told to us but should have been—whether they are stories of the Taliban in Afghanistan, how they were part of the Pakistan army and the human predicament which finds expression in my first film, *Kabul Express* or the story of 9/11 detainees which is what *New York* is all about,' elaborates Kabir.

But before we get carried away by his films, I steer him back to his pre-Bollywood days, and his experiences with the renowned filmmaker, Goutam Ghose best known for *Paar* and *Moner Manush*. Kabir used to freelance as a photographer for filmmaker Ramesh Sharma, who was commissioned to make a feature on Goutam Ghose. Later when Kabir and Goutam met to discuss the film, Goutam mentioned his plan about shooting his next documentary around the Silk Route tracing it from Bukhara in Uzbekistan to China through Central Asian Republics of Kazakhstan, Tajikistan, Kyrgystan, Turkmenistan and then Inner Mongolia and Tibet. Kabir was extremely excited at the proposal and after citing his previous experience in the Central Asian region, became part of Goutam's fifteen-member team which proceeded on a three-month long cultural and geographical journey in 1994. 'It was a dream come true, an amazing experience,' gushes Kabir as he was one of the first Indians to have traversed the route.

The documentary titled, *Beyond The Himalayas* was broadcast on Discovery channel and became a precursor for Kabir's long journey in filmmaking. After a two-year hiatus, Mahindra jeeps who were sponsors for *Beyond The Himalayas*, suggested a similar idea of a motor expedition from Singapore to Delhi retracing the Indian National Army's or Azad Hind Fauj's journey through Malaysia and Burma, to the Indian border. Goutam Ghose declined the project as he was busy with another film and instead recommended Kabir's name who added an interesting dimension to this historic journey and roped in two INA veterans, the late Captain Lakshmi Sahgal and Col Gurbaksh Singh Dhillon, to retrace the route through their perspective. 'Everyday of the shoot was magical! The two veterans were back after fifty-five years and hadn't ever imagined that they would return and rediscover people and places the way they had left and particularly, Burma which was, in any case, in a time warp. It was an experience that goes beyond words,' expresses Kabir.

The INA documentary was titled, *The Forgotten Army*, and after being screened all over the world, received rave reviews. Kabir would have ideally liked to make *The Forgotten Army* as his first feature film but it was *Kabul Express*, an autobiographical story which unfolded while shooting a documentary on the Taliban in 2001, that was destined to be his debut.

It was way back in 1996 when Kabir was commissioned by the International Committee of Red Cross to make a documentary about the post-war effects on the children of Afghanistan. He started the project and filmed for a few days but discontinued after failing to come to terms with the distressing stories of children in Kabul. Further, he and his crew members were forced to return to India after the continuous shelling from the Taliban camp, which was stationed about twenty kms outside the city. Within two months of Kabir's arrival in India, the Taliban had overrun the entire city of Kabul and the documentary had to be eventually shelved. However, five years later, and particularly in the post 9/11 scenario, when the Taliban regime was beginning to collapse, Kabir decided to revisit Afghanistan and shoot a documentary on the terror outfit, with his school friend and now line producer, Rajan.

'Because we were Indians, we couldn't go through the usual Peshawar route, so we flew to Uzbekistan. From there we drove to Tajikistan and tried to drive across to Kabul but got caught in an avalanche. A landslide, a chopper crash before we could even board, a river in spate – we faced all the possible difficulties and were literally at a dead end. Some nine days passed like this but on the tenth day, we got information from the Indian embassy that a very senior journalist was arriving and also trying to enter Afghanistan. The man in reference was none other than Saeed Naqvi!' he mentions impishly.

However, the situation in Afghanistan was extremely volatile, both politically and weather-wise, and after trying for seven days, even an influential journalist like Saeed decided to return to India. Meanwhile Rajan and Kabir decided to make one last attempt to check the local airbase and fortunately for them, a Russian military helicopter was scheduled to fly that day with supplies to Kabul and the two managed to convince the Russian military pilot to hide them in the cargo and fly them into Afghanistan. As planned, the helicopter took off, went through the Hindukush mountains and just outside the city of Kabul, the pilot suddenly lowered the chopper and asked them to jump off! (The opening scene of *Kabul Express* show the protagonists, John Abraham and Arshad Warsi jumping off a chopper.)

'So, what you saw in *Kabul Express* is exactly the way we had landed,' reveals Kabir. The reason for the pilot's midair adventure was logical. He couldn't have landed the military helicopter onto a civilian base and wasn't willing to bring it down completely as that would have moved him off the radar. After jumping off the helicopter in the middle of nowhere, Rajan and Kabir met an unknown Afghan who was on board a military tank (as means of regular transport), a common sight in the war-torn days, and made their way into Kabul. Kabir also reminded me about the scene in *Kabul Express* which was based on their experience in an Afghan jail with foreign mercenaries where they saw a hulk of a man, a dreaded Talib breaking into uncontrollable sobs while speaking on the phone with his family, which had taken him to be dead!

Even while directing documentaries, Kabir never lost sight of the big screen and began pursuing it aggressively when he realized that the documentary space in India was fast dwindling. Furthermore, he felt that these films were watched in a few elite exhibition spaces like the India Habitat Centre (IHC) or the India International Centre (IIC) in Delhi and the same suspects of 300-400 people would come to applaud his efforts. Although his documentaries found attractive buyers like NHK of Japan, Canal+ France and several such reputed media houses, Kabir had a deep yearning to communicate with the home audiences.

In the meantime, his wife Mini Mathur, the two had fallen in love at a shoot for one of the TV shows, was invited to Mumbai for the MTV VJ hunt and was selected even without going through an audition; such was her talent and appeal on the small screen! As her new job required Mini to spend fifteen days a month in Mumbai, a few months later, towards the end of 1999, Kabir also shifted base to Mumbai. Although he continued making documentaries, the big screen still beckoned and he doubly focused on refining the script of *Kabul Express*. As soon as that was accomplished, he started meeting people, some through Mini's contacts and others as he developed the leads.

'*Kabul Express* was a bit ahead of its time. Today producers are willing to take a chance with novel concepts because in recent years, the multiplex audiences have made such films successful. But in those days, there were barely two multiplexes in Mumbai and stories like *Kabul Express,* though praised by many producers, didn't attract funds, even from the so-called champions of alternate cinema.

'The only studio I didn't approach was Yashraj Films because of the stereotypes that we have in our minds; I thought Yashraj only made *chiffon romances* and love stories, and why would they be interested in a film like *Kabul Express*! If at all they did, they would make sure to add an item number in it, and so on and so forth. Also, no outsider had access to Aditya Chopra, he is like a ghost; no one is sure whether he really exists!' and with this, Kabir laid to rest the option of exploring Yashraj, only to be proven terribly wrong later!

One fine day, when Kabir got a phone call from Yashraj Films asking him to meet Aditya Chopra, he reacted predictably, "A cruel joke by one of my friends... just because I have been running around helter-skelter to find a producer!" However, after realizing that it was a genuine call, Kabir walked into Aditya's room at the appointed hour and experienced what he feels was one of the most surreal moments of his life—the reclusive, elusive Aditya Chopra was sitting across the table and began discussing the script with him, and most importantly, wanting to know when he could start filming!

But how did Aditya get to see the script of *Kabul Express*? I want Kabir to quickly clear the suspense.

It happened through a friend of Kabir's who was the line producer for *Dhoom* 1 (released in 2004) and was privy to the information that Aditya Chopra was not only looking for new subjects for Yashraj, but was also strongly contemplating starting a separate division to encourage such films in the future. (However it is another matter that the idea never came to fruition.) The friend therefore passed on the script of *Kabul Express* to Aditya who in turn discussed it with Jaideep Sahni, the writer of *Bunty Aur Babli and Chak De India!,* who was supervizing the proposed department. By yet another wonderful coincidence, Jaideep and Kabir happened to be childhood friends. Jaideep was in fact the first person to have read the script of *Kabul Express* and he obviously spoke well of his friend to Aditya and whatever ensued thereafter is now history!

Kabir had never imagined that he would be a feature film writer someday and was content as long as his pictures spoke louder than his words! And in so far as the script of *Kabul Express* was concerned, when Aditya asked him when he intended to start, Kabir openly discussed his plan to first hire a professional writer for the project.

'Adi told me that he was a very apolitical person and didn't follow international politics but felt there was something special in the script of *Kabul Express*… Whenever he needed any details about the backdrop, context and situation in Afghanistan, it automatically seemed to emerge from the script and he therefore overturned my idea of bringing in a professional writer! I became a writer by default,' chuckles Kabir.

As *Kabul Express* was being filmed, Aditya Chopra sprung yet another surprise on Kabir and signed him for an exclusive three-film deal with his company. To trust a first time director straight away with a three-film contract… Kabir is able to sense my bewilderment and offers an explanation, 'He probably saw a different, unique voice in my work… something that had the ability to break the clutter and stand out, that's why maybe…'

As it turned out, Aditya Chopra's judgement was indeed well placed. Finally, *Kabul Express* did exceedingly well—with a world premiere in Toronto, travelling to the London and Dubai Film festivals and finally to Busan at a time when Indian films were rarely showcased on international platforms. For Kabir the honors went a notch above when his film bagged the National Award (Indira Gandhi Award for the Best First Film by a director).

Kabir's next film with Yashraj was *New York*. How did *New York* come about? Was it the only script or one of the few that you suggested to Aditya, I ask.

'As a producer, Adi remains completely involved with the writing process as he was from the time I initiated the idea for *New York*. As you must know, the film deals with the subject of illegal detainees in the post 9/11 world and it intrigued me to such an extent that I had first started scripting it for a documentary much earlier, during the pre-*Kabul Express* days. Later, when I bounced it off Aditya, he suggested that we expand on the basic idea and make it bigger and more mainstream. That's how *New York* happened with John Abraham, Katrina Kaif, Neil Nitin Mukesh and Irrfan Khan. If *Kabul Express* was on the cusp of mainstream and alternate cinema—with no love interest, songs etc, in *New York* we incorporated these elements and focused on the masses.

'For a mainstream studio like Yashraj, a film on a controversial political issue was a big risk. Conventional wisdom says that mainstream cinema should be apolitical! Not only was *New York* very political, it was also set in a third country, so the risk was even bigger. Fortunately *New York* did extremely well at the box office and opened up further avenues for me,' shares Kabir elatedly.

For Kabir, the biggest take away from *New York* was to recognize the power of mainstream cinema. After filming documentaries on what may be called, "esoteric" subjects for several years, he was fully aware of what he describes as the "IIC syndrome"—preaching to the converted and not reaching out to the masses!

'Somehow that doesn't bring satisfaction. Mainstream is where one needs to play this game. The power and reach of mainstream cinema; the vast numbers you speak to, that's the fun….Ultimately you want to throw your ideas out to the millions and not to a select few in Mumbai and Delhi!' he states unequivocally.

Logically therefore, when it came to *Ek Tha Tiger*, the stars became bigger and the canvas expansive but the context remained like a typical Kabir Khan film. 'I believe that even though *Tiger* is my most mainstream masala film so far, it's also immensely political. If you read the politics of *Tiger*, you'll realize what I am saying—the top agent/hero of this country subverts the system and insists that love is beyond artificial boundaries that humans create! As a director, I can push that line but for a producer it was truly a courageous call to cast the two biggest stars of the country and make a film which a lot of people may view as subversive! All I can say is, hats off to Yashraj; it's been a great and very interesting journey for me,' he acknowledges.

So, what transpired that made him shift to Sajid Nadiadwala for his next film, *Phantom*?

Kabir replies, 'Yashraj was undoubtedly a safe haven for me. But I wanted to step out of the cocoon and see how big and bad the world can be,' he laughs and continues, 'there was no real reason as such except to experience something new, a sense of adventure, if I may say so!'

Kabir emphasizes that Sajid was also eager to produce different genre of cinema and hence the story of *Phantom* is far removed from the usual Sajid Nadiadwala films. It's an adventure drama which fits in somewhere between *Kabul Express* and *New York*, without a love story or the ubiquitous song and dance routine. 'The audience today recognizes the tone of a film. They expect songs in a film like *Yeh Jawaani*

Hai Deewani or in say, *Ek Tha Tiger* which was made with a mega star but in a film like *Phantom*, that may dilute the subject. I feel that *Phantom* will break new ground in the commercial-mainstream space,' he prophesies.

And how does the future look?

Kabir loyally goes back to his first love of photography and says that he would ideally like to strap his camera and get away for long periods to the remotest locales. However before he can do that, there are stories waiting to be told, many which will be embedded with a real connect, political context and definitely high adventure. Widening as it does the variety of Hindi cinema, we are surely not complaining!

'The power of cinema lies in the mainstream…..Ultimately you want to throw your ideas out to the millions and not to a select few in Mumbai and Delhi.'

IN HIS MENTOR'S FOOTSTEPS

KUNAL KOHLI

He is a dreamer, a believer and he is here for the long haul. Kunal Kohli thinks, breathes and lives cinema, the sole raison d'être of his life.

I first heard about the Think Fest from Kunal when he told me that we could meet after his return from Goa where he was invited to participate in it alongwith Amitabh Bachchan, Shekhar Kapur, Farhan Akhtar, Rakeysh Omprakash Mehra and Priyanka Chopra. Little did I know then that the Think Fest would dominate the news headlines for months on end and even as I write this piece, it is obvious that the entire context and the discussion around it is not likely to fade away any time soon.

So post Think Fest, in the second week of November 2013, I meet Kunal at his office located on the first floor of a residential building in Santa Cruz. Just like his movies, the décor in his room is also bright and chirpy, matched appropriately with the coolness of a sprawling green creeper decorating the French window just behind his work station. The cushions on a sofa opposite his desk loudly proclaim his love for the movies and are painted with scenes from classics of yesteryears—*Guide, Pyaasa, Kabhie Kabhie, Aaradhna,* etc.

Born in a middle class family to working parents who didn't exactly think of films as a future for their children, Kunal and his younger sister studied at the prestigious Cathedral and John Connon School in South Mumbai and were expected to be Management graduates. Kunal remembers that while growing up as a child, he would often wonder why they had to *write* compositions or stories and not draw them? Also how he enjoyed taking pictures for hours with an Agfa camera his mother had bought for him, and would end up spending all his pocket money on the activity.

After the tenth grade, Kunal joined H R College of Commerce in Mumbai whose alumni boasts of eminent peo- ple like Kumar Mangalam Birla, Gautam Singhania, Karan Johar, and Ruia brothers of the Essar group, etc. Like several other students, Kunal also suddenly felt liberated in college after the rigorous discipline of school and drifted aimlessly in the first year without a care in the world. But the following year, he made better use of time and started apprenticing at his uncle's sound recording studio. Soon thereafter, his uncle diversified his business and started a video editing studio and Kunal began assisting ace editors like the late Renu Saluja. By now he was completely fascinated with the world of enter- tainment and spent most part of his college dividing his time between studio work and academics.

Later, when most of his friends chose stable careers as Chartered Accountants, MBAs or managing family businesses, Kunal continued to hang out in editing bays where besides films, tv serials in both Hindi and Marathi were also being made. 'My parents couldn't understand what

I was doing in those studios. I was just an apprentice and was not even earning any money! But I would be out, assisting various filmmakers till late night. I also became a camera attendant and would go to the sets of various directors and help out in their work. A couple of years passed like this but I was nowhere near entering the film industry. I was still somewhere on the fringes. I even tried to produce a television serial for Doordarshan, the only broadcast channel at the time, but it didn't work out. That's when I started feeling the pressure. All my friends were working and I was still borrowing money from my mother,' he narrates about his floundering years in the industry.

Deeply dejected with his failure, Kunal decided—"I am not happening in this country, so *bhago*—run away to America"—to try his luck in the proverbial promised land. He found an accommodation in Manhattan with a little help from his cousins and took up a job that was most readily available to immigrants—that of a waiter and a bartender. He spent an entire year doing this and rose to be the maitre d' of the restaurant while managing to earn decent money for himself. But over this period he realized that this is not how he would like to spend the rest of his life and then one day, on an impulse which had gnawed him for weeks, Kunal packed his bags and came back to India. This was towards the fag end of the Eighties when India was on the threshold of economic reforms and was witnessing unprecedented growth in the television industry with the launch of several private channels.

This time around, Kunal got the timing right and after his return to Mumbai began working in programming for the now-defunct Plus Channel started by director Mahesh Bhatt and Amit Khanna, currently the Chairman of Reliance Entertainment. Even though he earned a meagre salary of three thousand rupees, the creative energy at his workplace, exposure to different aspects of programming and most importantly, a proximity to Mahesh Bhatt, someone he had admired for long for films like *Saaransh, Naam,* and *Arth,* was invaluable. 'I met Mahesh Bhatt at Plus Channel and it was love at first sight. I was a huge fan of Mahesh sahab. I loved his earlier films which to a large extent inspired me to be a filmmaker and I was lucky that I got to work closely with him at Plus,' he acknowledges.

Through Mahesh Bhatt he met several others he had once eulogized, like Sanjay Dutt, Subhash Ghai, Lakshmikant-Pyarelal, Javed Akhtar, Aamir Khan, Juhi Chawla and even worked closely with them on a tv show. The other and more pleasant encounter that Kunal had at Plus was with his colleague Ravina, whom he eventually married and she has been his close confidante ever since.

After an enriching two-year stint with Plus, Kunal moved on to the newly set up Zee TV Network which not only offered him a better salary, but gave him the freedom to design his own shows and he went on to do five programmes a week including, *Chalo Cinema, Philips Top 10, Kya Scene Hai, Sitara* and *Galaxy.* Of these, *Chalo Cinema* is still hailed as the pioneering show on film ratings, and was much awaited by audiences across India.

After thirty-six months with Zee and a tremendous track record of great shows, Kunal made yet another switch, and this time to UTV but only to feel restless yet again. It wasn't the work so much, as Kunal confesses, but rather the childhood desire to tell his own stories and after a year, he finally decided to work independently as a filmmaker. Even as he was mulling over his next steps, an unexpected offer made its way in the form of a music video from the prestigious Universal Music and the debutant Kunal directed the singer from UK, Bally Sagoo for *Mera Laung Gawacha* that not only became a huge hit but also bagged Channel V's Best Video of the Year award. In the next couple of years, Kunal monopolized the music video genre and directed twenty-seven chartbuster songs including, *Tere Bin Jeena Nahin* by Bali Brahmbhatt, the *Chui Mui Si Tum* series by Rajshri Films featuring Preeti Jhangiani and Abbas, Kamaal Khan's *Jaana*, and Shiamak Davar's *Jaane Kisne,* etc.

By now Kunal Kohli was ready to realize his ultimate dream but it unfolded in a manner which could have stymied his film career forever. A prominent film producer (whom Kunal desisted from naming) made him an offer to direct his next film, and before Kunal could celebrate the much await-ed break, severe strains began to emerge in their working relationship and reached a point when the two couldn't see eye to eye on anything. Meanwhile, for one of his freelance assignments, Kunal happened to interview Karan Johar on the release of his debut film, *Kuch Kuch Hota Hai*. He had in-terviewed Karan on an earlier occasion for *Chalo Cinema* and had known the filmmaker's illustrious father, the late Yash Johar because of the Mahesh Bhatt connection. He confided in Karan about his frustration and differences with his pro-ducer and the latter advised him to meet Aditya Chopra who at that moment was scouting for a director.

Although Kunal paid heed to Karan Johar's advise, he was diffident to meet the man he considered a genius and obviously after the stupendous success of *Dilwale Dulhaniya Le Jayenge*. However the two met and at first although Aditya shared his vision of starting a studio with Kunal, he also rejected his candidature saying he was only looking for fresh talent and someone who wasn't connected to the film industry in any way. And yet, somehow their discussion progressed and they soon realized that they shared the same wavelength. By the time the meeting came to an end, Aditya put forward a condition: Kunal would have to leave the film he had signed with the producer. Kunal asked him that if he did, would he sign him up for the project? Aditya refused to commit to any such proposition, and said that he would first work with him for a few days and then decide.

The meeting left Kunal in a conundrum. He shares, 'Till then, Yash Raj Films had never signed another director. It was solely managed by Yash and Aditya Chopra. I found myself in a weird situation. Aditya was not committing to me. The other producer had signed me and I knew that if we resolved our differences, we would be able to reach an amicable solution. I was totally confused! Should I still return the producer's money or go with Aditya who wasn't ready to commit...'

Kunal finally decided to return the signing amount to the producer but the latter, in an attempt to appease the young director, doubled the money and further confused him. Kunal narrates about his state of mind prior to joining Yash Raj, 'In the early 2000, when I met Aditya, Yash Raj was nowhere near what it is today. Of course it was big. It has always been but it wasn't the Yash Raj conglomerate with multiple studios, joint ventures and subsidiaries etc. That happened later and due to several factors and in a small way also because of my films. At that time, it was purely a family-run business albeit a highly successful one headed by one of my favourite directors, the legendary Yash Chopra. I was no less obsessed with Yash Chopra as I was with Mahesh Bhatt! Frankly, directors like Mahesh Bhatt, Yash Chopra, Subhash Ghai, Ramesh Sippy, Vijay Anand, and Manoj Kumar inspired me to become a director. And here I was sitting in the office of one of the greatest and being offered a job—there was this possibility of making a film with them—and I was not going to give that up for anything in the world. Over and above all else, I respected and connected with Aditya at different levels. I knew I could endlessly discuss cinema with him. So, at the end of it all, I decided to give it a shot and see if I could impress Aditya to sign me on. I started attending script sittings with him and enjoyed it to such an extent that soon I stopped caring whether he signs me or not. I actually stopped thinking about it,' says Kunal.

After 2-3 months, there came a day when it became obvious that Aditya was going to announce YRF's next film with Kunal as director and this was *Mujhse Dosti Karoge (MDK)* starring Hrithik Roshan, Rani Mukherji and Kareena Kapoor. Kunal recounts, 'Before we started shooting for *MDK*, I had given Aditya the rough script of *Hum Tum* and he asked me to go ahead with it first. But since we had the lead actors' consent for *MDK*, I was keen that we make *MDK* first. Finally *MDK* was released in 2002, didn't work at the box office but to my surprise, Aditya was totally unaffected by it and encouraged me to focus on the next which was *Hum Tum*. I was however a bit unsure because I had a feeling that perhaps *Hum Tum's* script was unsuitable for Indian sensibilities. Afterall a typical commercial Hindi film like *MDK* had not worked and here was Aditya wanting me to go ahead with this project—"*Karo, dekho kya hota hai* (Do it, let's see what happens)"—even though no one else in the company was in favour of taking such a risk. I learnt that a person who supports you unequivocally when you are down and out, wins your admiration and respect for life and that is what I have for Aditya – RESPECT!'

Contrary to Kunal's apprehensions, *Hum Tum* tasted remarkable success, both critically and commercially and was declared one of the biggest hits of 2004. The film won five Filmfare awards including Best Director for Kohli. It was also a landmark film for young Kunal because he was up against his mentor, the senior Chopra who was also nominated for *Veer Zaara* the same year! His next film with Yash Raj was *Fanaa,* released in 2006 and also became one of the biggest hits of the year and stood out for its lead pair's – Aamir Khan and Kajol's – fantastic performances.

Riding high on the consecutive successes of his films, Kunal launched his own production house in 2007 and for the first film under Kunal Kohli Productions, collaborated with Yash Raj Films to present *Thoda Pyaar Thoda Magic* in

2008. Although he repeated the *Hum Tum* pair of Saif Ali Khan and Rani Mukherji, they failed to recreate the old magic and despite a good opening, the film went unnoticed at the box office.

While Kunal's association with YRF was creatively fulfilling, was it financially beneficial? I ask.

Reveals Kunal, 'I never ever discussed money with them. I just couldn't and felt indebted that they had given me a break. I did four films with Yash Raj and took whatever they offered, whether it was less or more, didn't matter. It's not about the money. If I wanted money, I could have been a diamond broker. I remember at the time of finalizing the offer, their CEO, Sanjeev Kohli showed me the contract and asked me to go through it, show it to my lawyers, etc. I did none of that and asked him where I had to sign. He said they were giving me an X amount. I took that amount and signed. It was the same for my second and third film as well. They partnered with me for the fourth film, and in a similar manner I accepted whatever amount was suggested by them, and signed without any negotiations. I am not fabulously rich. You may find it hard to believe but I did my biggest hit films with survival money. However, what I certainly gained was priceless experience and some friends for life including Aamir Khan and Prasoon Joshi!'

And you also gained a definite place in the history of Indian cinema, I state!

With a sense of great pride and delight, he responds, 'I was fortunate enough to be the last director at Yash Raj to witness an era when the company made films as a family and for this I'll always be grateful to Yash ji, Aditya and Pam aunty. I was the first "non family" person to have become a director at YRF. The later ones can never imagine the kind of interactions I had with Yash ji. He was always part of my script readings and music sittings and I remember when we went to Switzerland for a recce, he came along and later accompanied us for the shoots. He was truly a father figure for the entire crew and very often Pam aunty would also accompany him and it was a norm for the whole unit to have dinner together and end the day on a happy note. Even though Yash ji was an extrovert and Aditya is introverted, they shared common passions for filmmaking, food and life, what the Punjabis are typically known for. I was no different in that respect and which is possibly why we got along so well.

'I saw the model of the studio in Aditya's room and then saw it being built. The first film shot in Yash Raj studio happened to be *Fanaa*. I sort of inaugurated the studio and was one of the founder members of the studio. That was a very happy time. Those memories are for life and have become part of YRF's history,' Kunal reminisces.

After *Thoda Pyaar Thoda Magic*, Kunal and Aditya parted amicably to pursue their independent working styles. On a personal level however, they continue to remain in touch, meet every year on Diwali, discuss films and have great conversations just like before. 'When Yash ji passed away in 2012, I was the first to reach his house. It was a huge blow for me. I was fortunate that I occupied a small part of his life. There are certain memories and events that you create with certain people which can never be replaced, erased or taken away,' says Kunal in reverence.

After setting up his own production house, Kunal Kohli produced two films – *Break Ke Baad* and *Teri Meri Kahaani* which didn't perform upto expectations. But he is not unduly worried and says, 'Filmmaking is a gamble. You never know what pays off and you learn from every experience. Sometimes there is no reason for either success or failure. You can't spend your entire life trying to analyze what went wrong! Smile at your success, smile even when you fail and move on,' he muses. And Kunal has truly moved on and to his next film titled *Vartak Nagar*, to be directed by

Atul Taishete in 2014. This time around, the story of his film revolves around four slum boys whose lives are impacted due to the Mumbai textile mill strike of 1992.

So, what is his yardstick for choosing his director, cinematographer, lyricist, and music directors?

Kunal explains, 'It's all by gut feel really and a factor of what appeals to you at that moment. In the case of Atul Taishete, it was his nine-minute-long film called *Rewind* which I saw and liked at a film festival in Stuttgart, Germany. He approached me and wanted to narrate a story to me. Initially I was reluctant because whatever little I had heard, sounded like arthouse cinema. But when I heard the script in detail, it came across as a heart-wrenching, hard-hitting story and I decided to back it, even though Atul has not made a feature film before. The one thing I learnt from Yash Chopra is that if you can write a subject, and narrate it well, you can also make a good film. Therefore, if I like the script and the person, I'll make a film with him. I met a lot of filmmakers at the German festival but Atul and I connected.

'As far as the choice of music director, lyricist and cinematographer goes, it depends on the requirement of the script; what I am thinking at that time, the feel I get from a certain person, someone whose work I have admired or someone with whom I have worked earlier and want to work again – one or more of these factors help me choose the team for a film. For my next directorial venture, I may work with an international Director Of Photography (DOP) because I want a very different look for a love story. So, there is never a set process or formula to it. Like I said, for me, it's just how I am feeling at that time,' explains Kunal.

Equipped with an illustrious past and pedigree, Kunal Kohli continues to have great enthusiasm for making films. In the past, he partnered with Reliance Entertainment and Eros for funding and at the time of writing this book, was getting ready to finalize a deal with the Sahara Group for his future projects. 'There is nothing, not one process of film-making that doesn't excite me,' he avers.

While with Yash Raj, he had helped promote one of his assistants, Siddharth Anand (director of *Salaam Namaste* and *Bachna Ae Haseeno*) by recommending his name to Aditya Chopra. He proclaims, 'I learnt from the best. I learnt how to nurture talent and to let go, how to step in when they needed help and step back when they didn't. I do exactly the same with my directors and hope I can reach the same level of success that Yash Raj had reached with me. It's an exciting journey and I feel it has just begun,' he smiles.

'As long as I am making films, I am happy, that's all I want to do. I am not a very religious person but whenever I ask for something from the universe, all I ask for is to let me make movies all my life. I want to go with my boots on, just like Yash ji,' he concludes like a true mentee.

'Filmmaking is a gamble. You never know what pays off and you learn from every experience. Sometimes there is no reason for either success or failure. Smile at your success, smile even when you fail and move on.'

THE PLAIN-SPOKEN PHILOSOPHER

MAHESH BHATT

I must have travelled countless times through the famous Linking Road in Mumbai and like most people, associated it primarily with shopping and restaurants. Today however, it revealed a completely new identity as a street that also has the office of Vishesh Films where I am headed to meet Mahesh Bhatt. As I enter the fourth-floor office located in Durga Chambers, a swanky building next to a Tanishq showroom on Khar Linking Road, I find that it looks every bit a new generation workplace.

Mahesh's chamber is tastefully done with black and white photographs featuring the "director in action" and has an adjoining movie theatre with a seating capacity for about thirty people. Dressed in his trademark casual cotton shirt and jeans, Mahesh is on the phone alternating between the Information and Broadcasting Ministry officials in Delhi and top cops in Mumbai about controlling a certain tense situation pertaining to some communally sensitive content on a television channel. That's the prelude to the conversation which is to follow with the philosopher-filmmaker who stands firmly for a pluralistic society in secular India.

As is well-known, Mahesh Bhatt has a staggering body of work to his credit. In a career spanning thirty years, he has directed fifty-five films, of which, *Arth, Naam, Janam* and *Saaransh* won him tremendous critical acclaim, and others like, *Dil Hai Ki Manta Nahin, Aashiqui, Sadak, Daddy,* and *Jism* took him to dizzying heights of box office success. His final directorial venture, appropriately marking the high point, was the autobiographical film, *Zakhm* in 1998 which won him the prestigious National Film Award for Best Film on National Integration as well as the Filmfare award for Best Story.

After he hung up his boots as director in the year 1998, Mahesh Bhatt, as they say, "kept his ear to the ground", minutely observing the likes, dislikes and aspirations of youngsters and has played the role of an able mentor. In an industry where star power reigns, under Mahesh Bhatt's visionary leadership, Vishesh Films opted to follow a diagonally opposite approach of working with new actors and thereby turning many like, Bipasha Basu, John Abraham, Emran Hashmi and Mallika Sherawat into "stars" in Bollywood.

How did he take to direction, I begin by asking him. Was it a compelling creative urge or simply because he was born to Nanabhai Bhatt, the Gujarati-Hindi filmmaker of the Forties?

As forthright and blunt as he always is, Mahesh replies in his inimitable style, 'The answer will demystify and destroy the halo artists carry of being special people who are possessed with this burning desire to create something special. The fact is that I was a bad student who barely went through school and dropped out in college. I was unable to deal with the boredom of a classroom and would daydream sitting by the window in class, finding life on the street far more exciting than lessons learnt by rote. It was pretty clear that I couldn't qualify for a job as a doctor or an engineer. Incidentally, those were also the days when my father had fallen on bad times. I was not very close to my father. Besides taking care of my mother, Shirin Mohammed Ali and six of us kids in Mumbai, my father had his "legitimate" family in Gujarat to take care of. So he had his own set of problems to deal with.

'I never leaned on my parents for either psychological, emotional or financial sustenance. I always saw myself as a person who should be responsible for my own life. So when I was fifteen, my mother asked me to work and somehow supplement my father's income and I began doing some odd jobs. A couple of years later, my cousin who was a close friend of Raj Khosla sahab (famous Bollywood director, producer and screenwriter who worked through 1950s till 1980s) helped me get a job as a production manager for *Do Raaste*. And from there began my journey in the world of films but only with the objective of making money. Some years later, I heard the great Charlie Chaplin when he was receiving the Honorary Oscar for his infinite contribution to the film industry. He was asked why he came to the movies and he replied that he did it for the money; people made an art out of it. I thought that was so honest,' says Mahesh candidly and further adds, 'Normally what makes people entertainers is not very different from what makes somebody a carpenter, doctor or an engineer.'

By the time Mahesh entered his Twenties, he married his school sweetheart, Lorraine Bright who later changed her name to Kiran Bhatt and when he was twenty-one, his first child Pooja was born. It was obvious that life was pushing Mahesh at a breakneck speed and even professionally, it did not take him long to make a transition from production to direction. Narrating the sequence of events, he recounts, 'It was in 1973 when my friend Johnny Bakshi, who was the production controller with Raj Khosla, asked me if I could direct a film. I remember I was the clapper boy. I had just given a clap for *Do Raaste* and I was still carrying the clap on my shoulder, when he summoned me aside and asked me this. Always having believed in firing first and aiming later, I promptly accepted his offer. Most importantly, I liked the idea of being the "emperor" on the set, which the director usually is.'

Whatever little Mahesh knew of cinema was by watching movies. The cinema halls became his classroom. Alongside, he also began reading about filmmaking and visited the American and British libraries to devour every book on cinema. As a natural corollary, he applied all this theoretical knowledge to his early movies and it wasn't much of a surprise when his first few films didn't work. Recalling his early failures, he shares, 'My Twenties were disastrous. I was married by the age of twenty, became a father at twenty-one and made a film that got banned.'[1]

Befuddled by the challenges that life threw at him and the failure of his films, Mahesh took refuge in drugs. To complicate matters further, he had an extramarital affair with the leading actress of the time, Parveen Babi, who was also lonely and vulnerable like Mahesh's mother and his wife, Lorraine.

The use of LSD played havoc with his consciousness and *opened* his mind to the mystical space. He took to ochre robes and became a follower of Bhagwan Rajanish aka Osho and remained his devotee for two and a half years. 'However, I was providing for my house through all this,' Mahesh emphasizes the point. 'I understood the importance of bringing food to the table. That way I have never abdicated my responsibility. I made ad films for Lifebuoy, Air India, Dalda, etc, to keep the body and soul together but essentially I was lost those days,' he confesses.

---

[1]*Manzilein Aur Bhi Hain*, made in 1974 was banned because it attacked the institution of marriage.

'While I was a Rajanish sanyasi,' continues Mahesh, 'someone told me about U G Krishnamurthy. He said there is this man who comes here, doesn't have an audience, doesn't give lectures but is an interesting person who debunks the spiritual search theory and is not a Godman. When I met him, I found him very radical. He completely negated the theory of spiritual quest and said this is the reality, this is the world that has good and bad days. There is no escape from the real world. The spiritual super market that you are shopping in, has wares that will not see you through life. You are a misfit in this ashram. Go to the real world and fight it out. One should make money within the parameters of society, adhere to rules and make one's mark. This is the only truth. The alternate reality does not exist.'

A new phase was about to begin in Mahesh's life. Conversations with U G Krishnamurthy delinked him from his "quest" and shaped his existence thereafter. The period also coincided with Parveen Babi's mental breakdown and complete collapse. That kind of left him totally altered.

Talking about his *resurrection* and a string of soul-stirring films that followed, he says, 'It is said that the ground you fall on is the same you use to stand up. So, in a way, my turbulent Twenties became the raw material and worked as a spring board for my new journey. I finally told the story of my own experiences in the 80s beginning with *Arth* which was a story told from the woman's point of view whose husband strays and the anguish she goes through.

'Later my own experience of getting into an extra-marital affair took away my claims of being a victim. I too had ended up doing exactly what my father had done. So far, I had thought I was being fashionable wearing my tragedy on my sleeve. I realized that was no tragedy. Yes, my father was not part of the narrative that was the narrative next door. We were aberrations in that space, but I did the same thing. So why was I judging him when the narrative I wished he had adhered to, was not operating in my own life? That's when I realized the duplicity in what we say and what we live. It was in *Janam,* which I made with Kumar Gaurav, where this insight is reflected. The character of Kumar Gaurav does not take an aggressive position as he understood that we are only human and victims of a certain cultural legacy that we inherit,' reflects Mahesh.

In the Nineties, as India witnessed the growing surge of satellite television, the middle class which was Mahesh's major consumer base for *Arth and Saaransh* kind of cinema stopped going to the movies. In what can be termed as the most significant business decision, Mahesh Bhatt understood the paradigm shift and focused on the young, under-twenty-five demographics in films like *Aashiqui, Dil Hai Ki Manta Nahin, Sadak, Sir, Hum Hain Rahi Pyaar Ke* and *Saathi.* The films were huge hits and Mahesh Bhatt was finally acknowledged as a great commercial success.

There was however this feeling of emptiness and restlessness that never seemed to leave him. After drugs, he took to alcohol—the helplessness of a drunk father was beautifully translated in his film, *Daddy* – and later gave it up for the sake of his daughter, Shaheen, from his second wife, Soni Razdan. Mahesh finally opted for work as the next sedative primarily to numb the noise in his head and his Forties became the most productive years of his cinematic career where in a span of a decade, he directed thirty-two films as well as two television serials. 'Work was my painkiller. I was working all the time, not so much for fame or the money but primarily because I didn't know what else I could do with myself!' he says.

One of the most significant watershed moments in the history of post-Independent India, the demolition of the Babri Masjid in 1992 and the riots in its aftermath left a deep impact on Mahesh. He realized that nothing much had changed in India since post-Partition; he was born two years later, in 1949. The Muslims were still being treated as "them" and he felt it was time to embrace the identity of his mother as it was not only an integral part of his being, but also reflected the essence of a secular and plural India. So even while he was experiencing the gradual waning of interest in making films, he made the last and one of the most defining movies of his career, *Zakhm*, dedicated to his sole inspiration, his mother.

Paying her a tribute, Mahesh states, ' I had seen a lot of life and all within my home. My mother was my greatest teacher. Although she wasn't openly forthright, she was with us in private. She understood that the world maintains facades and it is subterfuge that sustains the social fabric. So she maintained it to fit in, but led a life which was bold and very subversive from the point of view of traditionalists. She was unwed and a closet Muslim. She practiced her faith behind closed doors because in a country that had recently been partitioned along religious lines, she felt that this would protect her children. She gave us Hindu names, sent us to Jesuit schools, always told us that we were our father's children and were Brahmins. I could never see the reason why she did that! It was something I understood later… But I was hardly a person who was going to keep my life a secret. Whatever I inhaled, I exhaled. All this turbulence and dilemma of my childhood years finds depiction in *Zakhm*.'

According to Mahesh, *Zakhm* was also the bravest film he had ever made. 'Making it was nothing short of harakiri—in an environment where Right wing Hindutva forces had recently triumphed at the polls and were in power. In March 1998, the National Democratic Alliance or NDA had returned to power. A B Vajpayee was the Prime Minister and L K Advani, the Home Minister and mind you, Maharashtra was also run by the BJP and Shiv Sena. At a time like this, to make a film which openly attacked Hindutva elements was viewed by people as not just audacious but foolish! I did have my run-ins with the government and a problem which went on for three months with the Union Home ministry. But I persisted and made the film on my own terms,' says Mahesh with immense pride. And indeed, it was a fitting finale to an illustrious career. *Zakhm* won several accolades including the National Film Award for Best Actor for Ajay Devgn. Mahesh left the stage when the audience was still clapping and cheering, saying encore!

'But I had sung my song,' says Mahesh. He had turned fifty and his desire to make movies had finally withered. Moreover, he realized that life was going to be nothing more than a variation of the same thing. 'Sooner or later, there comes a time when you don't have any more films to make. Like a woman who can give birth to x number of babies, there are only x number of films that can organically sprout out of you, like the flowering of a tree. You may still continue to make innumerable number of films after that phase, but they are not extensions of your personality,' he reasons.

After *Zakhm,* Mahesh began his life as a producer and launched both actors and directors under the banner of Vishesh Films. One of their recent hits, *Raaz 3,* a horror-thriller directed by Vikram Bhatt did fantastic business of ninety-seven crores with a rank newcomer, Esha Gupta as one of the leads. 'Stars are created by us. We have touched so many lives. The new millennium has been a very challenging period for us. This is a far more invigorating phase. We have firmly maintained our position as part of the mainstream entertainment industry, weaving dreams and making products which can make people's lives a little interesting and insulate them from the harsh realities of the world. That's where I am now,' concludes Mahesh.

Voicing popular perception, I tell him how the class, sensitivity and finesse of *Saaransh, Arth, Janam, Zakhm,* etc, have been absent in the movies produced by him in later years and whether he also believes that the Eighties were the high point of his career?

The question gets an animated response from Mahesh and he says in his characteristic, defiant manner, 'I was here to make a living. I was not here to reform cinema, give some intellectual or emotional insight which the world was seeking at my door or to pander to my own needs of being a unique thinker or an artist. At the same time, this is also true that when I make a certain kind of cinema, it does not always mean that I subscribe to that genre. When I got into the world of movies, I was supposed to make movies for businessmen who wanted money from this vehicle. I couldn't assure them something and do something else! The so-called alternate cinema that I made and some people in the world choose to remember me by, like *Saaransh* and *Zakhm*, did not make money. But there is another India which doesn't even know about *Saaransh*. They know a *Sadak* and going by box office figures, there are far too many people who like *Sadak*. I have made both; they came from the same heart just like love and hate. I could oscillate between the two comfortably and found satisfaction in both. There are followers for both kinds of cinema. Why should people who like one kind have more grip over me than those who like the other?' asserts Mahesh refusing to get typecast in any particular mould.

I want him to share his insights; the unique quality that new and aspiring directors should have?

With the smile and deep composure of a man who has been there and done that, he says, 'I keep telling my juniors that if a dumb fool like me could become a filmmaker, you guys are very bright; you are cinema literate and you have it in you. It took me four films – rather four flops—to get to my first hit. The industry spent a lot of time training me but it trusted me. I believe that the emotional subtext of a filmmaker's life weighs heavily and bleeds into his work and exercises huge influence on the personalities of all those present on the set. So from a filmmaker's perspective, what's out of the frame is often more important than what's in the frame. In a globalized world, where the emphasis is on creating standardized products, what's going to be important is to hold on to your intrinsic unique attributes, your own cultural space from where you have blossomed. You have to be unique like for instance, Picasso who came and broke all the models but became a model himself. Be original, be authentic to your own nature, speak from your heart.'

And actors? How do they succeed in this intensely competitive space?

'They have to believe in their song for its uniqueness, a song that was never sung before. They have to be assertive to the extent that they feel they are the heartbeat of the universe! At the same time, they also need to know that the space they are occupying now was occupied by people before and if they just look back and glance at the lives of those who preceded them, they will learn a lot. That however cannot be their compass. Anyone's life cannot become a compass for the younger generation. They have to carve their own unique path.'

And how can an aspiring actor get to work with Vishesh Films?

'He or she can simply walk in,' he replies.

Are newcomers received well by production houses, I further want to know.

Mahesh does not mince words and says bluntly, 'Why the hell should the world roll out a carpet for you? This is an establishment which is committed to its own survival. So it will only use people who pander to its own needs.'

Does it give an edge to a person if s/he comes through a film school, I prod on.

'Institutions polish pebbles and dim diamonds. So whether those who have come from the institutes are polished pebbles or dim diamonds, I don't know. I didn't go to a film school. There are also a lot of people who went to film schools and came out with a great data bank as an asset and have risen despite the albatross of organized education. Organized education is a data bank. If you look at it from that prism, as something which is available to you for ready recall, it's fine. But the danger is that these schools start teaching students about the greats which results in a tendency in an aspiring filmmaker to stifle his own voice and it may take him a lifetime to hear his own in the din of those who were greats, the likes of Satyajit Ray or Raj Kapoor. You start believing that their voices are so important that you don't listen to your own! Instead you start speaking in their voices. But we don't want to hear their voices, we want to hear *your* voice. It takes a lot of time and guts to speak in your voice,' he sums up.

Is there an expectation from the young entrants to follow a certain code of ethics in Bollywood?

'There is no code of ethics. You are only here to use me as a spring board for your career. We are co-travellers. We meet at a point in life. In fact the youngsters who have come and contributed to my company have left me richer. So to say that it has been a one-way traffic where they alone have gained, is not true. I have gained much more from them.'

Why does India's quest for an Oscar remain elusive?

'The fact is that our minds are still colonized. It seems as if the western parameters are the only measures to gauge your worth. China has refused those yardsticks and has made tremendous impact. So I think India needs to wake up and understand that only if you cater to an indigenous audience, will the world wake up to you. If you want to go and stand at the altar there, you shall be rejected. In fact, they want to use you to come here. The big boys from Hollywood are here. They want to touch the rickshawallah on the streets of Jharkhand and leave their brand with him! 20th Century Fox wants to enshrine itself in the *jhopris* of Mumbai and wants to use us as a spring board. They are not interested in my climbing the altar at Los Angeles, the mecca of entertainment, the platform for the Oscars. Only if I make a film that catches the world's imagination will I find a place there. And I certainly cannot capture the world by abandoning my personality. That's how the greats have made a mark for themselves. The Lifetime achievement award was given to Satyajit Ray. Why? Because he made films which pandered to his taste and were sourced from his background. The guy was shaped by Shantiniketan and had Tagore, Vivekananda and the greats resonating in him. He did not imitate Martin Scorsese or any other filmmaker in Hollywood. He did it by remaining himself, and which took him to that great altar.'

What about educating your children in the best cinema schools? And when you have the means to do so?

'You know what's the greatest gift my daughter, Alia Bhatt gave me when her picture, *Student of the Year* became successful? The day I came to know that the movie had opened brilliantly, I asked her like a proud father to give me her first autograph and she wrote me a great note which said, 'Dear papa, thanks a million for not helping me at all during the making of this picture. I love you very much.' By not extending any help, I made her realize that she is complete on her own. What makes me very happy about the achievements of my children is that they did it on their own terms. They fumbled, they fell, they got up—that's the way I learnt and that's the way they will learn. I'll be there to talk to them, chat with them, nurse them, console them, inspire them, but walk, they shall have to on their own. So what I teach my children, I tell the world. I do not want to give you crutches. I want you to realize that you have the legs to stand on. Look at this girl, Shagufta Rafique… She came from the streets, was a bar dancer, singer and she wanted to write! Today she has written *Murder, Jannat, Raaz* and *Aashiqui 2* – all are stupendous hits. She didn't go to any film school. She learnt through life and has nourished my company with her raw vitality and tremendous street smartness. Story telling skills don't belong to those who go to some New York school of cinema. My daughter was studying in Jamnabai School and one day she went and acted. Karan Johar gave her the role after putting her through fire. There was no recommendation. Her schooling begins now. I learnt filmmaking by making films. The formal school is one's life, it's the work we do, the school is the crucible of public verdict. No filmmaker comes into his own without being squashed by public verdict. People teach you, your faults warn you. I pray that everyone faces disasters early in life because it gives you a kind of shock and makes you realize that you are human. Otherwise you think you are God's special child, blessed with some great talent and that you will be insulated from ordinary life. Therefore to fail is of great importance. That's why I often say, the only times a great writer delivers is first, when he is heartbroken, and second when his heart is overflowing. When I wrote from a broken heart, I made *Arth* and when I wrote from an overflowing heart, *Saaransh* happened. Talent doesn't belong only to people who go to universities where the tendency is to intellectualize; it's raw life that resonates—a simple human story, that's what filmmaking is all about,' are the final words from the master of the craft.

Having navigated the challenges of changing times well, there is no doubt that Vishesh Films will continue to play a key role in Bollywood. If the patriarch of Vishesh Films, Mahesh Bhatt was to make a directorial come back in this dynamic environment of today, it's easy to guess that it will be from an "overflowing heart" and it will indeed be interesting to see his masterly take on "life in the intervening years" since his last outing, *Zakhm*.

'Talent doesn't belong only to people who go to universities where the tendency is to intellectualize; it's raw life that resonates—a simple human story, that's what filmmaking is all about.'

'INDIE' SPIRIT PERSONIFIED

NAGESH KUKUNOOR

I feel Nagesh Kukunoor is one of the most articulate, eloquent and original film directors India has had in contemporary times. Born in Hyderabad in a family far removed from films, Nagesh led an extremely *dramatic* life to fulfill his deepest desire to be a filmmaker.

I met him in June 2013 at the office of Shreya Entertainment, in Andheri West which produced and distributed his film, *Mod* (2011) starring Ayesha Takia and Rannvijay Singh. He had just wrapped up his latest project, *Lakshmi*—about a child sex worker, and was scheduled to travel abroad for its release in select film festivals.

Nagesh Kukunoor was born in the late Sixties and grew up in a middle class Telugu family with an elder sister and a younger brother under the care of extremely supportive and liberal parents. His father gave up his job with the state government and later joined UNICEF, while his mother remained at home to care for the family. The Kukunoor children met their parents' expectations and did well in academics. 'We were the ideal middle class Telugu family. I became an engineer, my brother a doctor and my sister who has a Master's degree from the US, worked in the corporate sector for a while and then veered off to teaching,' states Nagesh.

However, apart from academic brilliance, there was something very special about young Nagesh. His family and friends remember him for his extraordinary story telling abilities which would magically unfold during the sweltering summers of Hyderabad when they would huddle indoors to escape the cruel sun. Nagesh would either narrate the stories of films that he had seen or would spontaneously concoct something for his audience. Later at high school reunions, he would often be reminded by his classmates about the way he would stand at the head of the class and not only narrate the stories of *Don* and *Sholay* but also enact scenes from these cult movies!

Nagesh did three years of schooling at the reputed Montfort School in Yercaud, Tamil Nadu, amongst whose alumni include, Dr Shashi Tharoor and cricketer, Roger Binny. Therefore it was no coincidence that Nagesh's second film, *Rockford*, in 1999, was inspired by his experiences in the boarding school and was shot in his alma mater.

After finishing school, Nagesh opted for Chemical Engineering at Osmania University as he was insistent from the beginning that not only did he want to study at the best university in Andhra Pradesh, he didn't want to live away from home. And as promised by his father at the time of entering college, Nagesh was gifted a Hero Honda motorbike, one of the first in Hyderabad! 'I had the coolest parents. I had my set of keys to the house and had complete freedom to come and go as I pleased. Right from the time I turned fifteen, dad allowed me to have a drink as long as it was at home. Once I got into college, I was allowed to go out drinking. So it was that kind of a ridiculously liberal and generous home where nothing was taboo. The basic rule was that no questions would be asked as long as we did well in academics!' recalls Nagesh.

In the Eighties, an increasing trend had engulfed the universities in Andhra Pradesh, and which remains unchanged even in 2014. Every student in the state dreamt of working and living in America and Andhra Pradesh at one time had the distinction of sending the maximum numbers to the US. Nagesh was no different but there was yet another compelling reason that found support for "destination US" in the Kukunoor household. Nagesh's father's boss in UNICEF was an American and he had set an example by practicing what was most uncommon in the India of the Eighties—insisting on being called by his first name (even though Kukunoor senior had joined as his personal assistant), lending his swanky Renault and Peugeot when Mr Kukunoor could only afford a modest cycle, etc. Simply put, from a very young age, Nagesh believed that America stood for liberty and equality and as a smart student in AP, the decision was made rather easy.

When the time came for him to leave, it happened with clockwork precision! He applied to several universities in the US and succeeded in getting a full scholarship to Georgia Tech, one of the premier engineering schools located in Atlanta in the State of Georgia. He now arrived in a place which he had always loved, thanks to Hollywood films and therefore, once he touched the American shores, he was sure this is where he belonged and would never return to India. 'Look at the irony. My brother was very clear that he would do his specialization in the US but definitely come back to India. He has stayed on while I am the one who came back,' quips Nagesh.

He continues, 'I can't describe what America did to me. Suffice to say that it shaped me into who I am. There is something about the air which tells you that you can be whoever you want, whenever you want; you can change your mind twenty times over; there is no wrong or right or the *only* way. There is something magical about that place that breeds entrepreneurship and free thought. That kind of thinking and philosophy is what I gravitated to and I am so glad that I actually incorporated it in my life as it is easy to be enamoured by a philosophy and appreciate it from far, but tough when it comes to adapting it. I came across many examples of people from middle class backgrounds with a typical "safe approach thinking", who later went on to change tracks and became filmmakers. That made me think: why can't I do the same? But from experience I can say that the process of mustering courage to switch fields is not easy and takes a lot of time,' proclaims Nagesh.

And while these radical thoughts often crossed his mind, he stuck to his middle class "safe approach thinking", followed the conventional safe route and picked up a decent job after completing his Master's degree, which was a stepping stone for procuring a green card. 'Those were very exciting days. At each step, there was anxiety and fear that this would bring an end to one's time in the US,' he shares. However, everything moved very smoothly for Nagesh and he was able to procure a suitable job, sponsorship, work visa and also the coveted green card.

As early as three years into his professional life and Nagesh started feeling unfulfilled. 'Unhappiness is a great motivator. If you are a happy human being, you never look at doing things which are radically different. Most of us take leaps of faith when we are really unhappy and have nothing to lose. Despite money, success and all that I aspired to achieve, having been checked off, there was this deep rooted unhappiness which wouldn't go away. The next steps in the conventional scheme of things would have been to acquire an MBA and get married. I shuddered to think of my future. My biggest fear was that I would wake up one day and realize I was in my Forties, had a wife, a house, two kids and a dog and that would signal the end of my dream!'

This is exactly the direction in which things had started moving for him when he was reminded of a pact he had made with a close friend at Osmania that included a Master's in the US, a job, a few years of work experience and then an MBA from Harvard. His friend invoked the promise and prompted him to start preparing for the GMAT examination. Nagesh, obviously in a conundrum, thought that if he ever had to take the tough call, it was now – to step out of the conventional bogey, as it were, else it would be too late!

Although he can't recall exactly when filmmaking became his cherished dream, a few friends from his B Tech days remember that after a few pegs down, he would routinely say, '*Mujhe kuch aur karna hai* (I want to do something different).' As the first baby step in that long journey, he confessed to his friend that his heart was not in pursuing an MBA and left it at that. He had resolved that his dream was his "secret" and believed that he would rather do something than merely talk about it. It was obvious by now that by declining to do an MBA, Nagesh had started on an irreversible journey that would take him closer to his goal of being a filmmaker.

However, he had no clue where to begin and between experiencing mixed feelings of anxiety and adventure, he started out with film manuals and in the process located the Rockport School of Film Workshops, in the state of Maine in Northeast US, which held workshops round the year for filmmakers, television professionals and artists. Nagesh utilized a week of his annual vacation to sign up for the workshop and landed in Maine. 'It was there that I felt ALIVE. It was a workshop on film production and I saw video cameras, dollies, equipment, boom mikes for the first time ever… For that one week, I felt like I was in heaven. I remember vividly how I came back brimming with excitement to take a plunge into the new world that had opened up in front of me and beckoned me with an immense pull. I felt completely ecstatic. And then,' he takes a pause and I expect to hear how his life took a turn from here. 'And then… I did nothing!' he says!

A few months later, his parents came to visit him and one fine day, over a biryani meal cooked by his mother, he finally told them, 'I want to do something different…' His father responded, 'Hmm… An MBA, finally!' Nagesh nodded his head and said, 'To the contrary. I want to do something with the movies!' Although this came as a shock for his parents, after a short silence, they acquiesced even though they wished Nagesh wouldn't veer off so drastically.

But then once again, Nagesh did *nothing* and went back to his daily routine. 'In a fit of energy, it's easy to say stuff but to finally take that step is very difficult,' he shares his musings.

In the meantime, he signed up for a modeling workshop in Atlanta as that was the best he could find around the city which did not have much to offer in films and media studies. At the workshop, although he was appreciated for his *ethnic* looks, nothing really came to fruition, other than some small, insignificant assignments.

As a norm, in the American showbiz industry, an artist is asked to take his headshot in black and white and on the reverse carry his/her resume. One day when Nagesh went to get his resume printed at one of the few such copier machines that were available, a lady kept staring at him and commented that he had an interesting and expressive face and if he had ever considered acting? She then handed over her card to him carrying details of the Warehouse Actor's Theatre and suggested that he should give them a call.

Nagesh casually slipped the card into his pocket thinking that it might be another money making sham and forgot about it.

A couple of months later, on a very frustrating day, even as he was fretting over his unassertiveness, he suddenly remembered the lady at the copier machine who had handed him a card with a number. Nagesh immediately began a frantic search, and called the number only to be confronted with an answering machine at the other end. The following day however, someone returned his call and asked him to meet up for an interview.

It was destined. The Warehouse Actor's Theatre would change Nagesh Kukunoor's life forever. He started studying acting under one of the finest teachers of the craft, Judson Vaughan; after attending office from 9-5 pm, he would dash off for acting lessons from 6-10; stay on for rehearsals after the classes and sometimes well past midnight. If there was a local shoot, he would request to be included in the crew. Furthermore, Nagesh also managed to be represented by a reputed agency in Atlanta and bagged a few assignments, albeit small and even worked as an extra in others where he would often be required to wait upto twelve hours for a small appearance. But despite such frenzy, there wasn't a moment when he felt either stretched or drained out. This period of self-discovery was turning out to be the most significant phase of his life. By now, he had also come to terms with the fact that everything he loved and cherished so far, would have to be sacrificed at the altar of cinema. 'I was in many relationships but none of them lasted. Whenever it reached a particular point, say after about three months or so, an alarm bell would go off in my head and I would break up. I was terrified that it would interfere with my dream.'

But you could have always tried co-opting your loved one into your dream! I say.

Nagesh reveals the gentle side of his persona at this juncture and explains, 'The only person you can control is yourself and sometimes it is not possible to even do that. I was terrified that I'll have to worry about the other person too. The guilt of sabotaging her dream, so that she could participate in mine, disturbed me. Instead I would pre-empt it and step out of the relationship. When I look back, without doubt I was in love with some of the women I broke up with. I truly had some wonderful relationships which ended for the same reasons.'

While precious relationships fell by the wayside, Nagesh ended up studying acting at Warehouse for close to three years. Finally in the year 1995, Nagesh quit his job and decided to return to India with the conviction that in the international context, his "Indianess" was a unique factor and decided to make movies at home for showcasing in the west. Very clearly, another compelling reason was that making movies in India was also more affordable. The first place where he announced his decision to be a filmmaker was his acting school and Nagesh was euphoric when his classmates cheered and applauded and treated him like a star. However, the good feeling lasted till the next morning when he woke up in a cold sweat out of fear! But he had resolved to go through the motions and remained supremely conscious to not get dissuaded and in a dramatic move, gave away all his furniture and emptied the house leaving no scope for any amendments. In the next few days, he wound up pending tasks, transferred all his savings to India, boarded the flight and landed in Hyderabad with a singleminded resolve to finally be a filmmaker, but with no concrete plan in hand!

Once home, as a first step, Nagesh decided to use his training as an actor to get some work and also hoped to assist some directors in order to learn the craft, as was the norm. He circulated his portfolio, that he had made in the US as a model and actor, to agencies and even travelled to Mumbai to scout for some opportunities. Meanwhile, a friend of his knew some inconsequential actors and producers and Nagesh even met a few but all of that came to naught. Finally, through an acquaintance, he managed to get on the set of a serial that was being shot in Hyderabad called, *Veer Hanuman*! However, within a few days of working on the set, he concluded that he was unsuitable for this genre of programming—with Sita sitting forlorn under a tree with garish make up – as it clashed with his overall sensibilities.

He drew up all the courage within him to reinforce the reason that had brought him back to India in the first place–to make his own film. Afterall he was an engineer, had managed several big projects; a film could also be approached like a project with a defined budget, resources and timelines, he reasoned. As the next step, he went into complete isolation, locked himself up in a room and wrote passionately for an entire week. At the end of seven days, the script for his first film, *Hyderabad Blues* (HB) was ready. Next, with the help of a cinematographer friend he had met on the sets of *Veer Hanuman*, he planned a tentative budget but it soon became apparent that unless he went back to the States and worked for approximately a year and saved every penny, he wouldn't be able to launch the film.

Nagesh called one of his clients in Atlanta, who had once offered that if he ever quit his job as a consultant, they would be happy to hire him and in no time found himself sitting on a plane to America. The job at hand was a dream, comprising extensive travel around the world, a fantastic salary, attractive perks, amazing growth prospects and Nagesh could sense that it also had the potential of detracting him from his goal. 'This is where fate tests you; do you really want it? *Do you really want it?*—that's what fate was asking me,' remembers Nagesh but also that he was determined and kept his new apartment empty except for his luggage and a new TV set. The last test came in October 1996, when at a swanky hotel in the upscale Martha's Vineyard in Massachusetts, while celebrating the company's success, he announced to his Vice

President that he was leaving. His boss sat him down and advised that he should not rush the decision and explained the bright prospects in terms of promotions, salary hikes and stock options. That night Nagesh lay in his bed thinking that if he worked for three years with the organization, he would be able to make his movie at a fraction of the amount he would earn at this company, but that was not to be.

Shot in a short span of seventeen days, Nagesh's debut film, *Hyderabad Blues* was released in 1998 to much critical acclaim and became one of the most successful independent films and inadvertently also jumpstarted the Indie film movement in India. Besides receiving the Audience award for best film at both the Peachtree International Film Festival in Atlanta and Rhode Island International Film Festival, it was showcased in several distinguished international festivals as well.

Every frame of the "success sequence" that Nagesh had often dreamt for his debut film, came to fruition exactly in the manner in which he had imagined; much similar to the way it had unfolded for the American independent filmmaker, Edward Burns who wrote, directed, produced and acted in *The Brothers McMullen* in 1995. Made on a shoestring budget, shot largely in his family home in Long Island in America, *The Brothers McMullen* had created waves at film festival circuits and was subsequently picked up by 20th Century Fox, one of the leading Hollywood studios, for distribution. This is the recipe Nagesh followed: to make an independent film, take it to a film festival, get positive reviews, have a distributor watch it and buy the film, and then release it as a huge commercial success.

'Back in those days it was and still is the path for an individual who has no backing,' he comments.

Hyderabad Blues was followed by *Rockford* (1999) which opened in the Austin Film Festival ; *Bollywood Calling* (2001) premiered at the first London Film Festival; *3 Deewarein*

(2003) was released to much acclaim at various international festivals and went on to bag the Filmfare Award for Best Story. Amongst his later films—*Hyderabad Blues 2* (2004); *Iqbal* (2005); *Dor* (2006); *Bombay To Bangkok* (2008); *8x10 Tasveer* (2009); *Aashayein* (2010); *Mod* (2011) – *Iqbal* stands out as a magnificent film which also received the maximum laurels. Of the rest however, *Aashayein* unfortunately, got embroiled in a dispute between distributors and could not be released and *8x10 Tasveer* suffered due to inadequate marketing efforts by the producer.

Despite a robust filmography, Nagesh remains undeterred about his original plan to exclusively showcase his movies for the international market; his recent film, *Lakshmi* (2014) also followed the trajectory of his debut, *Hyderabad Blues* – which was to screen it at various film festivals abroad before releasing it for the Indian audience. For a man who gave up his career twice over to chase his celluloid dream, nothing seems like a real challenge any more, except exploring new creative frontiers through his films!

'Unhappiness is a great motivator. Most of us take leaps of faith when we are really unhappy and have nothing to lose.'

Nandita's association with cinema began way back in the year 1995. She has since acted in over thirty feature films in ten different languages and has won accolades for her bold and sensitive performances in films like *Fire, Earth, Bawander, Before the Rains,* etc. She also turned director with *Firaaq* in 2008 which won her several national and international awards. Yet another important milestone in her career was her stint as the Chairperson of Children's Film Society of India (CFSI), from 2009-2012.

As soon as I return from my annual visit to the UK, coinciding with my son's new session at the university, I meet Nandita at her beautiful 7th floor residence at Worli. The main door of her home leads to the hall that has the dining set up at one end and a sit out at the other which lends a stunning view of the Arabian Sea stretched out for miles. A glass door opposite the sit out separates the living room and the office space. Beautiful paintings, plants and books largely make up the earthy and lively décor of Nandita and her husband, Subodh Maskara's residence-cum-office.

It's an early morning meeting. The house is abuzz with a battery of helpers attending to various chores and making sure that tea and breakfast is laid out for the couple and their guests. While Nandita and I begin our conversation in the living room, Subodh goes about his day's work with his associates.

Born to the renowned painter and sculptor, Jatin Das and eminent Gujarati writer, Dr Varsha Das, once Director of the National Book Trust and National Gandhi Museum, Nandita grew up in a liberal family in Delhi with her younger brother, Siddhartha. 'My brother and I were fortunate to have parents who let us do what we enjoyed doing. They never exerted pressure on us. I don't remember them ever using words like career, success, money, ambition. These words were not part of our vocabulary,' she shares.

Recalling her childhood, she narrates, 'I didn't enjoy Maths very much and if I was anxious before any exam, my father would ask me to relax, water the plants and talk to them and that seemed to really work in calming me down and getting my concentration back. He encouraged me to continue with my Odissi dance classes even during my board exams!' she exclaims. Her diligence and the supportive environment at home yielded wonderful results and she topped her school, Sardar Patel Vidyalaya in Delhi.

Unlike Maths, Nandita loved Geography in school and chose to pursue it later in college at Miranda House, Delhi. During her first year in college, while Delhi University faced a major shut down due to a teachers strike, Nandita got an offer through her parents' contacts for a small but pivotal role in *Parinati* directed by Prakash Jha. At the time, the role happened to be a pleasant coincidence and Nandita went along without giving it any serious thought and in fact, signed up her next acting assignment only a decade later!

'Interestingly, moving images were not exactly part of my growing up years. My parents rarely ever watched any movies. Going to art exhibitions, theatre, music and dance performances was something we all did. Even a television set came home eight years after it had come to all other households that we knew of,' she says explaining how films were so far removed from her horizon.

Even though academics remained the focus for Nandita in college, and she scored brilliantly, she gradually began devoting considerable time to both dramatics and Odissi, which she had learnt for twelve years. But it was *nukkad natak* or street theatre which seemed to obsess her completely for the next few years. After a chance introduction by a classmate who was a member of the Jana Natya Manch or JANAM founded by the late Safdar Hashmi, the well known playwright and activist in the Seventies and Eighties, Nandita became fascinated with theatre and more importantly, as an effective tool for social change. She was invariably assigned the lead role and performed with the troupe all across Delhi – in colleges, public spaces, slums, and even in factories. This exposure laid the basic foundation for her future involvement in various socio-political issues.

By the time she completed her graduation, one thing became clearer that it wasn't going to be Geography any more! Meanwhile, uncertain about her next course of action, Nandita decided to take a year off to teach at the Rishi Valley School in Andhra Pradesh, founded by the eminent philoso- pher, J Krishnamurthy. The teaching assignment also gave her the freedom to explore the country and life seemed to be beautiful until January 1989 which heralded the new year with the terrible news of Safdar Hashmi's brutal murder by political goons in Ghaziabad (UP) while he was performing the play *Chakka Jam* with his troupe in support of workers' rights. Like several others, Nandita was completely jolted by Safdar's untimely death and as a tribute to her first *political* guru, decided that she would pursue a path that would keep her directly engaged with people and social causes.

After bidding adieu to Rishi Valley School and a life which gave her the freedom to steer it any which way, Nandita enrolled for a Masters in Social Work (MSW) at Delhi University. The course included two days of field-work every week and at the end of two years, an intensive Block fieldwork spanning two months. Nandita chose to spend her first year college vacation also towards such work at a Gandhian organization near Bardoli in Gujarat. Her second Block fieldwork was at a remote tribal village in Phulbani district in Orissa (in today's Kandhamal district) and involved dealing with tribals and environmental issues, in utterly primitive living conditions. 'It was not too much of a culture shock for me as we were used to spending a month of our summer vacations every year in Mumbai, which was my mother's natal home, and one month at Baripada, my father's village in Orissa. In a way, I straddled two contrasting worlds with ease, and that made me more flexible and less judgemental,' she comments and continues, 'The MSW course affected me deeply, not because a degree makes you a better or worse social worker but it just exposes you to different social realities. I realized that what I took for granted was not the norm in the society at large, the world out there being quite different and harsh for millions of people.'

As a natural progression, Nandita went on to work for a couple of years with NGOs engaged in women and children's issues till she was offered *Ek Thi Goonja* by film-maker, Bappa Ray whom she had met in Kandhamal during her fieldwork. The film revolved around a poor, tribal girl who educates herself and fights for the rights of her community. Nandita gladly agreed to do the role and at the time saw it more as an extension of her social work. 'Films happened completely by default like most things in my life. *Ek Thi Goonja* was a small "festival film" which won some awards, was shown on TV and then faded away. Finally, it wasn't even released commercially. So, *Fire*, which I did next, was in a way my first film. After *Goonja* I didn't think I would do another film but the role in *Fire* was not only interesting but very compelling. Even though ours was a very liberal family, homosexuality was not really discussed at home. I understood it intellectually, but not emotionally. *Fire* exposed me to how we perceive the "other"–someone who may not be like us, and also our deep rooted prejudices and conditioning. Therefore, my experiences of working on human rights and my street theatre days instinctively made me gravitate towards subjects and stories that were related to people's dilemmas, and relationships. And my work on gender issues helped me understand women characters better and the need for them to be real and layered. I feel fortunate to have played a range of women characters,' she elaborates.

Although Nandita later acted in a couple of mainstream Hindi films like *Aks*, *Pita*, *Supari* and ensured that her roles in these films were meaningful, she felt disillusioned with this space and the repetitive experience of essaying such roles and turned to regional films, which she felt were far more satisfying. Also the commercial Hindi film set up was too hierarchical for her liking.

So did she enjoy working in regional cinema, particularly in South Indian languages?

Though she admits she has a flare for languages, she confesses it wasn't easy to work in Malayalam, Tamil and other South Indian films. 'It's a different sort of pressure one faces when you do films in languages you don't speak. Besides worrying about the way one portrays a character and emotions, you have to focus a lot on learning the dialogues. It was like an exam for me and I would swear not to subject myself to another such film. But then an interesting story, a wonderful director would come by and you forgot everything; it's like the memory of a pregnancy!' She quips.

So what else compels her to sign a film? I ask Nandita.

'More often than not, I have chosen to do a film because of what it wants to say, a story that needs to be told. I look at acting as a vehicle, a larger platform through which I can communicate with people about the various causes I feel for,' she sums up about the sole motivation that drives her acting career.

And how did the transition to direction happen, I ask.

'At a stage when I had acted in over twenty films, and during some shoots that didn't turn out the way I had expected, I would often fantasize about directing a film! And I started working on a script about a couple's relationship. But somehow, *Firaaq* was meant to be my debut film. After the 2002 Gujarat riots, I was deeply disturbed, like many of my friends. Though I didn't visit Gujarat for months post the riots, I heard, read and also saw for the first time on television, what one had so far only imagined about the Partition. I began to think deeply about "identity" and the notion of the "other". I started delivering a series of talks on this theme and the interactions would invariably tend to get very heated and polarized. There would be so much venom and a feeling of "them" and "us". After a series of such talks, I felt that I needed to do something that would not only be cathartic but also become a vehicle to share my thoughts about the subject with a larger audience. And this resulted in *Firaaq*, a story set in the aftermath of the Gujarat carnage in 2002, when all the obvious violence had abated and there were residual emotions of anger, regret, guilt, retaliation, and emptiness....'

Nandita had initially thought of writing *Firaaq* as a single, seamless story but changed her mind after she visited Gujarat and broke it down to multiple stories that brought

out several human emotions and the dynamics of relationships in troubled times. Therefore organically it became an
ensemble film and once all the stories were in place, in order
to discipline herself in writing the screenplay, she brought
Shuchi Kothari, her friend from Auckland on board with
whom she had earlier done a short film in New Zealand.
Shuchi, apart from being a Gujarati married to a Muslim, was
a perfect fit as she taught screenplay writing at the university
level in Auckland. Nandita and Shuchi first wrote the screenplay in English and Nandita later translated most of it into
Hindi and the process went on for three years particularly
because Nandita had to divide her time between her acting
assignments and advocacy work. Once the screenplay was
ready, Nandita handpicked each location and cast members.
'I think I wouldn't have been able to direct it if I had not
written it. Because I was so close to the subject and involved
in every aspect that I was able to put it all together,' she says.

As a next step, Percept Picture Company was brought
on board as the producer, an experience which turned out
to be quite unpleasant for Nandita. There was not only
very little support from the production company, they also
failed when it came to marketing and distributing the film.
Under such circumstances, though the entire process of
filmmaking seemed very stressful to Nandita at that time,
in retrospect, she feels that she emerged stronger and richer
after the experience. 'If they had been amazing producers, I
would have learnt much lesser,' she says and reiterates that
everything happens for a reason. However as a director, she
cherishes having worked with a range of actors—stalwarts
like Naseeruddin Shah, Paresh Rawal and Deepti Naval
on the one hand and on the other many who were from a
theatre background and facing the camera for the first time.
Nawazuddin Siddiqui, who later won people's hearts with his
sterling performances in *Kahani* and *Gangs of Wasseypur* was
first spotted by Anurag Kashyap in *Firaaq*.

For a debut film as a director, it was commendable that Nandita shot it in exactly thirty days, as planned and precisely within the budget laid out for it. Apart from the content of the film, what was equally important for her was to bring a non-hierarchical approach to the whole process of filmmaking. 'Much of my work has been about bridging the gap, whether of gender, class, caste and the same attitude was brought to filmmaking, and we followed a no-frills-plain-work format whereby all the cast and crew lived in service apartments, ate together and were treated equally,' she throws light on what she means when she says that the process was as important as its outcome.

Finally when the film was released, it generated debate, got several rave reviews, travelled to the very prestigious Telluride Film Festival in Colorado where the who's who of the international film fraternity including Danny Boyle watched the film. Next was the Toronto Film Festival, followed by Vladivostok in Russia, Busan in Korea, to Durban, Istanbul, London, Singapore and Pakistan, etc., and was lauded at every platform! 'That was exhilarating, almost like an affirmation that human emotions and predicaments are universal. Every place had an "us and them" story, episodes of sectarian violence destroying people's lives, which is what connected *Firaaq* to audiences across the board,' infers Nandita and continues, 'The film festivals were a catalyst and I presumed that my film would get enough publicity at home. For me it was most important to show it in my country but sadly, it was not marketed well and could not reach out to large numbers. Thankfully, in this day and age of the internet, cinema has a longer shelf life than just a theatre release, so luckily through Youtube, DVD and satellite rights, it has managed to get a longer lease of life.'

What's her take away from direction after starting out as an actor? I want to know.

She responds promptly, 'Direction is a different experience altogether. It's the most challenging thing I have ever done. For me, it was the coming together of all my passions and was almost like a spiritual journey. You deal with so many people, it's as if you take on the role of a parent. As actors, you are only privy to your part of the shoot, which is a small sliver of the filmmaking process. I feel actors are perceived to be much larger than they really are. But direction is far more challenging and fulfilling. I had the opportunity to tell my own story, my way.'

Soon after *Firaaq*, Nandita met Subodh Maskara through common friends and after a few months of courtship, decided to get married in 2010. What films couldn't do, marriage did and she finally relocated to Mumbai.

In the same year, she was asked by the then Information and Broadcasting Minister, Ambika Soni, to take up the responsibility as Chairperson of the Children's Film Society of India. Nandita had always been interested in children and felt that it was a good opportunity to develop alternative entertainment options for children and accepted the demanding assignment. 'It was not easy to work in a structure that had existed for fifty-five years and was heavily bureaucratic, with several archaic rules and defunct regulations. It needed many systemic and creative changes,' she comments.

Under the circumstances and within the available resources, Nandita involved various filmmakers, animators, writers, school teachers, parents, children and other stakeholders to participate in CFSI's activities. Eventually her efforts paid off and in 2012, she managed to release CFSI's first film in its fifty-five years of existence called, *Gattu*. Though she was asked to serve another term as Chairperson, Nandita declined the offer as she wanted to spend time with her son, Vihaan who was born just after she had assumed the responsibility at CFSI and through the first two years had deftly juggled her responsibilities as a mother and as Chairperson, a purely honorary assignment to which she had committed.

After a whirlwind few years since the making of *Firaaq*, Nandita recently returned to acting and finished shooting for Soumitra Ranade's film, *Albert Pinto Ko Gussa Kyon Aata Hai*, in the same vein as the original with the same title directed by Saeed Akhtar Mirza in 1980. Next on anvil is a Spanish film that was first shot in Mumbai and then in Barcelona, where reel life imitated real life by way of Subodh playing the role of her husband! However, this wasn't the first time for them as they had earlier played a married couple in their theatre presentation titled, *Between the Lines*.

Going forward, Subodh is focusing on their company Chhoti Production's theatre venture called Cineplay, which is aimed at digitizing plays and making them accessible to more people. Meanwhile Nandita has also found a story for her next film and wants to focus on it. 'This is just the beginning and its fruition will take a long time, but at least the journey has begun,' she comments.

'To not make the mistakes I made in *Firaaq* and to tell another powerful story that needs to be told. Frankly, I now want to completely dive into the writing process,' confirms Nandita. 'I will continue to act because I believe that acting requires much less time and energy and has its own charm. It is also a good way of keeping in touch with the medium. You meet different people, you become a part of different stories and most importantly, it gives me the platform for discussing issues which are close to my heart,', says Nandita who chooses to be a humanitarian first and everything else later – an actor, director, writer, columnist—ever evolving and open to whatever else is coming her way, provided her heart beats for it!

'I feel actors are perceived to be much larger than they really are. But direction is something that is far more challenging and fulfilling.'

THE SOFT-HEARTED REBEL

PRAKASH JHA

I have an early morning meeting with Prakash Jha. His office, tucked away in a lane just off New Link Road in Andheri West close to Fun Republic cinema hall, wears a quiet and sombre look at this early hour. At the reception, large-size posters of his latest release, *Satyagraha—Democracy on Fire*, peer at me curiously. The housekeeping staff is getting the office in fine fettle before the rest of the executives arrive. Through the reception, I enter a big hall which is filled with the beautiful fragrance of incense from the small pooja altar that has, besides the pictures of gods, a framed photograph of Prakash's mother. There are fine paintings, sculptures and artistic furniture strewn all around, which look enchanting in the morning light shimmering through trees outside.

Prakash is seated at a small table in his study which is at one end of the hall, separated from the rest of the area by a low swinging wooden door. Our conversation begins over a cup of green tea, and by the end, I realize that I have got converted into a bigger admirer of the talented director.

Born in a farming family in the west Champaran district of Bihar, bordering Nepal, Prakash is the eldest son, followed by a younger brother and a sister. His father, who had the rare distinction of being one amongst the only three graduates in the village, was employed with the state government. Both his parents were ambitious – his mother wanted Prakash to join the Indian Air Force–and wanted the children to pursue academics. Therefore, as a nine-year-old, after a couple of years in a nearby school, Prakash was sent off to one of the best known boarding schools in the region, the Sainik School at Tilaiya in district Koderma, in today's Jharkhand. As is apparent by its name, the school groomed students from an early age to enter India's defence services.

The environment at the Sainik School seemed extremely constraining to Prakash and more so because he would often question traditional norms and frequently face punishment. However, his academic performance helped him to sustain through the rigorous routine and finally qualify for the National Defence Academy (NDA) examination after class ten.

But two factors stymied his defence ambitions. First, and what was obvious from the beginning, his deep inclination towards the fine arts, which often kept him occupied for hours and second, his growing disdain for wars or any other kind of violence. Therefore despite clearing the coveted NDA exam, Prakash stood his ground and refused to join the esteemed institute. After several days of intense discussions, Prakash's father was left with no option but to transfer him to another school. He took his son from one school to another for the entrance exam and in the process, Prakash lost a year, and finally appeared for his class twelve exams from Central School, Bokaro and fortunately scored impressively.

As a natural corollary, it was now expected of him to continue with academics in the science stream and qualify for one of the IITs! Just in case it didn't work out, the alternative was to become a scientist or a civil servant. Prakash's interest in subjects like History were considered irrelevant particularly when he was good in both Maths and science, and he did eventually end up joining Physics (Hons) at a college in Delhi University.

As a college student in Delhi, Prakash was totally thunderstruck by the historical city's open spaces and unending beauty. 'From a fenced and cocooned life in school, both physically and mentally, where one lived by extreme discipline, the timetable, here I was in a world where I could easily hop into an autorickshaw, go to Connaught Place and watch a James Bond movie or with friends to a disco, smoke if I wished to and even drink — all of which was unimaginable in school,' reminisces Prakash. While exploring the capital city, he would often discover exhibitions either in Mandi House (home to the National School of Drama), Ravindra Bhavan, the Sangeet Natak Akademi, Sahitya Akademi, Shri Ram Centre for Performing Arts, or the Triveni Kala Sangam and would be mesmerized. In the culturally vibrant city, his eyes would catch everything artistic—paintings, sculptures, different crafts or even buildings and he would often stand in front of M F Husain's huge mosaic fresco adorning the WHO building and imagine that some day he would also be part of such beautiful things in life!

Alongside all these attractions, college and Physics classes also rolled by. However, after the first five or six months of his first year programme, Prakash finally realized that he wasn't inclined towards formal education and conveyed it to his parents. 'It was difficult for my parents as it would be for any middle class family where parents do their best. It weighed a lot on them. It took me the next couple of months to keep talking to my mother and convince her that I wanted to do something else. She just didn't understand my point of view! And I don't blame her, after all every parent has aspirations,' narrates Prakash.

As the final exams drew near, Prakash went back home during preparatory leave and after mustering up all the courage, confronted his father and declared to him point blank, 'Enough is enough; I don't want to become an IAS officer. I don't know what I want to do. I want to find out. Maybe I will become a painter or something…'

And after this face-off of epic proportions, he didn't go back to the university and his family which was immensely shocked, decided to leave him behind in the village and moved to another location somewhere in south Bihar, where his father had been posted. Prakash was now all alone in his ancestral home, and took care of the farm and oversaw the crops. 'This was the time when I felt like a complete outcast. Everyone thought that *yeh toh barbaad ho gaya, khatam ho gaya* (he is destroyed, finished),' relates Prakash.

The Jhas' ancestral village house in Bihar was fairly large with a lot of space in and around it. Prakash decided to convert the backyard into a sort of workshop and started making sculptures and mostly idols of goddess Durga or of temples consecrated in her name. His latent interest in the arts and particularly in sculpting had finally found expression in the lonely village home and helped him to firm up his mind to study at the J J School of Art in Mumbai. He decided to meet his parents one last time and after handing over the responsibility of the village house, came to Patna and boarded a train to Mumbai with just three hundred rupees in his pocket. The year was 1972 and he was a young lad of nineteen!

On board the train to the city of his future dreams, the young Prakash Jha was noticed by a fellow passenger called Rajaram who had boarded the train in Jaunpur (UP) and observed how Prakash was managing frugally with some *chana* and tea. After several hours, when the train passed through Bhopal, Rajaram offered to share his lunch with Prakash and by the next morning, they had become good friends. Rajaram was a labour contractor for the Oberoi chain of hotels and left his visiting card with Prakash saying, '*Agar tumhara kuch thikana nahin hai toh mere paas rah jana* (If you don't have a place to stay, you can stay with me).'

Rajaram owned a building in Dahisar (the last mile within the Mumbai Suburban District) of which he had rented most flats but had also retained a couple for people who worked with him. Prakash moved into one of those flats, sharing it with 10-12 people who had also been offered accommodation by Rajaram. In return for the favour, Prakash had to visit the site where Rajaram worked and maintain a record of attendance and accounts everyday for a couple of hours.

Very soon, Prakash visited the J J School of Art but was told that he would have to wait for a few months for admissions to begin. Alongside working for Rajaram, Prakash would continuously look for extra work and came across an advertisement requiring English tutors by an institute in Kalbadevi area (an old time business district for traders and buyers in Mumbai, close to the Chatrapati Shivaji Terminus–CST). Prakash was hired to teach spoken English to Gujarati, Marwari and businessmen from other communities. Kalbadevi had several such institutes that ran classes through the day and Prakash made enough money to sustain himself. 'I wasn't a spendthrift those days and got by each day with the barest minimum, mainly for food and bus fares. Initially, there were days when I went without food but it was fine. Somehow, it never bogged me down and I could manage,' says Prakash detailing the struggles of his early days in Mumbai.

Amongst the co-habitants of the building owned by Rajaram at Dahisar, there was also an art director who was well known for his glass work and had to his credit the epic film, *Mughal-e-Azam*. One day, he saw Prakash taking a picture. 'I had bought a camera from Nepal, which was located very close to my village. Those days, we couldn't find good cameras in India. I remember, it was a Yashika camera…' shares Prakash and continues, 'The art director liked some of my pictures and we became friends. Then on a Sunday, I accompanied him to the set of a movie which was being shot at Sun N Sand hotel in Juhu. None of these hotels – J W Marriott, Centaur, Holiday Inn, etc., existed then. Hotel Horizon, which is a site under construction today, where Rajesh Khanna and Dimple got married, also didn't exist. The film under production at Sun N Sand was called *Dharma* and the cast on the set included, the late Navin Nischol, Pran and Rekha. While my friend was talking to the director, I stood in a corner and keenly observed the goings-on and was mesmerized with the whole environment – the lights, cameras, set, the costumes, etc. The director of *Dharma* was a gentleman called Chand Bhai. His eyes suddenly met mine and I asked him politely if I could stay on the set for some more time? He nodded a yes and I stood in a corner for nearly nine to ten hours at a stretch, trying to be invisible! I didn't move out because I thought if I did, they won't let me in again. On that day, a *qawwali* shoot was in progress and I saw an entire sequence. As evening turned to dusk, I had made up my mind that this is exactly what I wanted to do in my life. My friend and I went back to Dahisar and I asked him if he could formally introduce me to Chand sahab which he happily did. I could manage a place as an assistant with Chand Bhai. I was his thirteenth assistant and the job did not involve anything more than just being available to him and bring him a glass of water or a cup of tea and some such errands.'

By the end of the four-day shooting schedule, Prakash realized that if he continued to be Chand's assistant, it would take him twenty years or more to become a director as there were several other assistant directors who had been in the same position for a decade-and-a-half! Prakash clearly didn't have that kind of patience and decided to join the Film and Television Institute in Pune for a formal initiation and training. In the India of those days, where even telephones were a rarity, Prakash travelled to Pune to make enquiries and found that admissions to the institute – which involved a written test and an interview— would be held after a good ten months or so. Prakash thought about the ten-month hiatus and his prospective admission and was deeply worried about his financial crisis. There was no question of asking his parents for help. At the time of leaving home, his mother had nudged his father to give him some surplus money, but he had stopped her and said conclusively, 'Ma, I don't want him to pay for something he doesn't want me to do.' Besides funds, there was one more factor which posed a hurdle. The FTII made a graduate degree incumbent for any candidate wanting to pursue a direction course at the institute. Prakash obviously didn't have one and was given an alternative of doing a two-year course in editing which only required a high school degree. But Prakash couldn't procure even that as he hadn't appeared for his school leaving exam in Delhi and didn't have the certificate for that year! Finally, after all the travel and struggle, the FTII dream was relegated to the backburner.

Once he was back in Mumbai, Prakash Jha decided to leave Dahisar and live around Juhu and Santa Cruz area where several film shootings took place. He made friends with some bhelpuriwallahs and chaat vendors on Juhu beach and managed to sleep in a niche within their stalls for some months. Alongside, he once again began scouting for work and this despite his job with director, Chand Bhai. The reason was that as a rule those days, only senior technicians were qualified as assistants and they were paid a meagre amount sufficient for a one-time meal! Others like Prakash, who was the thirteenth assistant, was paid a mere five rupees a day for all the hard work.

A few days later, Prakash came across an advertisement for the position of assistant manager in a restaurant in Colaba. Although he knew nothing about restaurants, he decided to take a chance by going for the interview. As luck would have it, his interviewer and owner of the restaurant was also from a Sainik school in Kapurthala and Prakash was hired. Since his job was in the kitchen and required him to report early, he was also provided accommodation in a guest house which was next to Regal cinema, in Mumbai's Colaba Causeway. 'It looked like a common room with a few beds, separated by plywood partitions. The cubicle I got was exactly 4 ft by 6.5 ft, barely enough to fit a bed and get in,' recalls Prakash. He would be the first to reach the restaurant everyday and get the kitchen going by sanctioning the masalas, meat, poultry and other ingredients. 'It turned out to be a great experience as I learnt cooking,' states Prakash, finding a silver lining in difficulties. There were additional free hours during lunch time when Prakash was not required to stay around the restaurant and he decided to resume his studies at the neighbouring K C college. He discussed his situation – of holding a fulltime job—with his teachers who supported him fully. Prakash began his classes in History and Social Sciences and would sometimes also bring packed food for the teachers! At the time of the final examinations, he also managed to get a place in the college's hostel at Churchgate and passed with good grades.

Meanwhile, the hostel accommodation proved to be a boon for Prakash in more ways than one. Behind the Churchgate station, in the AIR building, there used to be a non-commercial cinema hall called Akashvani which would screen arthouse films from India and abroad. 'So we could watch films by Satyajit Ray, Mrinal Sen, etc. I became a regular there and started getting attracted to parallel cinema. I remember seeing *Distant Thunder* (*Ashani Sanket*) by Ray for seven consecutive nights!'

Whatever Prakash earned, went into savings as his food and lodging were taken care of and he was anyway a man of few needs. Very soon, he had collected enough money to pay for FTII, Pune and joined the institute which was at the time headed by the noted film director and actor, Girish Karnad. However, one year later, after the students staged a massive agitation at FTII, they were asked to leave and Prakash returned to Mumbai, once again with no place to live!

With whatever little experience he had gained at the FTII, Prakash now began applying for documentary films and sponsorships, when someone introduced him to Shashikala Kakodkar, the then Chief Minister of Goa, who after viewing some of Prakash's photographs sanctioned him a film on the theme of 'Harmony through Goa Festivals.' This was a yearlong project which showcased different festivals of the state and therefore, at the time of one, Prakash would travel to Goa and be back in Mumbai to wait for the next one. Finally, the documentary film was done, and as was the norm those days, was exhibited in cinema halls before feature films. Amongst several other things, one of the fall outs of this project was that Prakash never went back to the FTII and hence didn't get his diploma.

A few days later, at the invitation of some of the independent filmmakers he had met in Goa during the filming of the documentary, Prakash travelled to Germany and was away from the frenetic pace of Mumbai for a while. A pleasant surprise awaited him on his return as his parents had come to visit him after five long years! It was obvious to Prakash that his documentary on Goa had reached the theatres in Bihar. Although Prakash had made it a point to keep his mother informed of his whereabouts, he never went back home to meet his parents during his period of struggle.

Meanwhile Prakash continued directing corporate and documentary films and also started applying for work at the Films Division and Children's Film Society in Mumbai. Soon, he was commissioned a long-format documentary on the life of a ballet dancer in India which took him to Russia and the UK in the late Seventies-early -Eighties and the two years in London proved to be a turning point in his career. 'Filmmaking is an instinct that cannot be taught. An institute can only guide you,' believes Prakash. Further, he also became a regular at the Notting Hill Gate cinema in London which showcased arthouse classics. 'For the price of one ticket, it was possible to watch two great films in a row. It was a place that reverberated with energy. People could smoke and drink in the hall and the atmosphere used to be charged with animated discussions amongst filmmakers,' remembers Prakash. Prakash's routine invariably involved watching films till the wee hours of the morning and then jog back to his apartment, catch some winks and be ready for work again during the day.

His first film after returning from London in the early Eighties was a documentary titled, *Faces After the Storm* and was based on the communal riots in Bihar Sharif. The riots had broken out while he was still in London and he remembers how after landing in Mumbai, he had handed over his luggage to a friend, taken a taxi and headed straight to the Films Division office. 'N S Thapa was the Chief Producer at that time and he gave me a unit when I told him that I wanted to go and do this documentary. We got on to a train and went straight to Bihar Sharif. By then, although the riots had subsided, the scars of the aftermath were still visible. The documentary was well appreciated and I won the National Award for it. With this, a new chapter began in my life.'

By now, Prakash Jha was insistent on making a feature film and found it in the script of *Damul*, which was set in feudal Bihar. Strapped for funding yet again, while he approached the National Film Development Corporation (NFDC) for *Damul*, he started working with Manmohan Shetty on *Hip Hip Hurray* starring Raj Kiran and Deepti Naval in 1984. Just when *Hip Hip Hurray* got over, the funding for *Damul* came through and things began to fall in place. After *Damul,* came *Parinati* and a documentary on the classical dance forms of India and Prakash was soon feted as one of the most promising filmmakers of the time.

However, towards the beginning of the Nineties, at a time when Indian economy was opening up to the world, Prakash Jha began to feel somewhat disillusioned. 'The funding from NFDC had almost come to a stop. It was difficult to make low budget cinema and recover costs. The mainstream commercial cinema required big budgets and was a genre I was not comfortable doing. Also there was an upheaval in my personal life. I was married to Deepti (Naval) but our marriage was not working,' he explains.

As a result, Prakash moved to Delhi for some time and directed the popular television serial, *Mungeri Lal Ke Haseen Sapne,* and a documentary called *Moments,* on Pandit Govind Ballabh Pant's life, for Doordarshan, a film in which the then Prime Minister Rajiv Gandhi took personal interest as head of the committee that had sanctioned the project. However, neither relocation nor television could bring inner peace for Prakash and he decided to quit the film industry. He moved back to Patna and devoted himself to social work by setting up an NGO called Anubhooti which not only initiated people towards film appreciation, the culture of cinema and its technique but also spread awareness about disaster management, flood relief and worked towards the overall welfare of the region. The involvement with social issues however came with a cost. Over a period of time, it depleted all his funds and unfortunately coincided with his father's retirement. Worse was when his mother passed away and he was faced with raising his adopted daughter, Disha, who had been in her grandmother's care so far. Very soon, with a four-and-a-half-year old girl-child in tow, empty coffers and no roof over his head, Prakash came back to Mumbai after a gap of nearly five years!

As a first step towards rebuilding his life, Prakash rented a place in Andheri West in one of the MHADA (Maharashtra Housing and Area Development Authority) houses. In the last five years, the entire cinematic narrative in Mumbai had undergone a paradigm shift and the only way to survive was by adapting to the commercial formula. In order to get a foothold in the industry, Prakash began by working on a mainstream masala film called, *Bandish* starring Juhi Chawla and Jackie Shroff. Midway through it, he started work on *Mrityudand* (which he had conceptualized prior to his return to Mumbai), based on women's emancipation in rural Bihar, something that was closer to his oeuvre and the film heralded a new phase in Prakash Jha's journey as a filmmaker who became adept at combining his cinematic sensibilities with box office success, and went on to win various awards. Several such films, particularly on socio-political themes with a big star cast followed in quick succession viz., *Gangaajal* (2003), *Apaharan* (2005), *Rajneeti* (2010), *Aarakshan* (2011), *Chakravyuh* (2012) and *Satyagraha* (2013; which he was in the process of making when I met him). Meanwhile, *Rajneeti 2* and *Gangaajal 2* are slated to be released in 2014.

How easy or difficult was it to get an an actress like Madhuri Dixit for *Mrityudand?* I am curious to know.

'Madhuri was doing *Khalnayak* (released in 1993) when I approached her for playing the lead in *Mrityudand*. She heard the script and agreed instantly. I was fortunate that she trusted me and accepted the offer. *Mrityudand's* success gave me a lot of credibility in the commercial cinema circuit. I am glad I enjoy the trust of actors like Ajay Devgn, Amitabh Bachchan, Ranbir Kapoor, Arjun Rampal, Manoj Bajpayee, Deepika Padukone, Katrina Kaif and Abhay Deol, who have worked with me,' replies Prakash in his measured soft tone which to me seems in sharp contrast to the high octane movies he makes.

Prakash also contested two Lok Sabha elections from Bihar in 2004 and 2009, respectively. What made him turn to politics and would he contest again in 2014?

'The dismal state in Bihar, prior to Nitish Kumar becoming the Chief Minister, drew me towards the idea of bringing social and political change through politics. I gave myself ten years to make a positive impact on a mass level through politics and contested the Lok Sabha elections in 2004 and 2009. The second time around, I came close to winning and lost by a very thin margin. I think it was a tactical mistake to not have contested as an independent candidate (he was fielded by Ram Vilas Paswan's Lok Janshakti Party). As regards whether I will contest the next general elections – no, I wont! I am already sixty and there are other things which are high on my priority list. As far as social intervention is concerned, I will continue to do that through my organization, Anubhooti. We have a strong base in the region and besides the regular social, cultural and developmental work, we have carried out large scale rehabilitation operations for people affected by the floods. We are building a hospital now. The first mall and multiplex of Bihar has also been built by me in Patna which is in the second year of successful operation. It's called P&M mall after me and my partner, Manmohan Shetty. We are building another one in Jamshedpur which will be operational soon.'

What keeps you going and what are your plans for the future, I ask.

'Post 2015, I want to slow down and do the things I have always loved like, painting, music and also learn to fly a plane! All my office work is concentrated in this very building. The CEO and CFO of the malls sit here and the editing, sound recording and all other work related to my films is also carried out from here. My father stays in Patna and has been devoted to Vipasana meditation for the last twelve years. There are many people who come and meditate with him. He is like a guru to them and there is always a lovely ambience around him. I spend two to three days a month with him and talk to him every day. But for these last twelve years I have not sat with him for any session. I wish to do that some day. My father laughs and tells me that my work is my meditation. It's a job that requires concentration. For example, the script of *Satyagraha* is going through its fifth round, the set for the film is being fabricated in Bhopal, the shoot schedule has to be planned, the costumes have to be done, songs need to be recorded; the team managing the malls want closure on the design for chairs, the restaurant, the security men need a couple of more bouncers! So, I am busy and charged up all the time! Every single day in the last forty years, since I left home, has been exciting. I have never had a day when I felt I had nothing to do. I know no other way to live but to live and enjoy each day,' avers Prakash with a zen like calm on his face.

Suddenly in the middle of the uninterrupted, long conversation with Prakash Jha, I now begin to hear the increasing din of office sounds. Prakash's daughter, Disha has also arrived. After completing her school, she started working as an assistant in Prakash Jha Productions. Today, the office is going to be busier and more crowded than usual as the casting unit is holding auditions for some roles in the forthcoming movies.

It's time for me to bid adieu to Prakash to enable his team members to get his attention. As I leave the company of a very fine director and an affable person, it is with the thought that I have to catch him at direction, at crafting the magic, another day very soon.

'Filmmaking is an instinct that cannot be taught. An institute can only guide you.'

THE EFFERVESCENT DREAMER

R Balakrishnan, popularly known as Balki, holds a unique distinction. He is not only a successful Bollywood direc- **R BALKI** tor, producer and screen writer, he is also the Chairman of Lowe Lintas, one of India's largest advertising agencies. He shot into instant fame after the success of his directorial debut, *Cheeni Kum*, followed by his second and highly appreciated film, *Paa*. In 2012, he produced *English Vinglish*, directed by his wife Gauri Shinde, which won the duo accolades both in India and abroad.

I look forward to meeting Balki this afternoon as I drive towards Express Towers at Nariman Point in Mumbai where Lowe Lintas' office is headquartered. While I wait for him to arrive from his meeting at Hindustan Unilever Limited, one of Lintas' oldest and key clients, I get a splendid view of South Mumbai's business district from his expansive 15th floor C-suite which is sparsely furnished. Conspicuously visible right down below through the glass pane, is a slightly arched and elongated building of Life Insurance Corporation's (LIC) head office. It's as if LIC is a constant in Balki's life—I discover this later as I get to know more about the distinguished director.

It's not too long before Balki joins me and his arrival instantly fills up the room with a lot of energy. Dressed as usual, in a black, semi-formal shirt and jeans, his face covered with a thick stubble, he seems to "represent" the creative world which refuses to fall in line with the conventional power dressing norms followed in the corporate sector and one that believes in a certain personal style and power of ideas!

'You are meant for advertising,' were the words of Balki's first mentor, Dr Naganand Kumar, Head of Human Resources at Mudra, who selected him way back in the Eighties to train in Ahmedabad. However, a career in advertising was not a conscious choice for Balki. It was more like "stumbling upon" something unknown and discovering it as he went along.

Balki was born in Halasuru (earlier known as Ulsoor) located in central Bangalore (now Bengaluru). His father worked with LIC and his mother taught at a nearby school and later became its principal. Right through school at Frank Anthony Public and later while pursuing B.Sc. from Christ College in Bangalore, his focus remained more on cricket and films than on academics. He was introduced to the magic of cinema very early in life at home, by his father who was a film buff.

'The first film I saw with my father was *Julius Caesar* starring Marlon Brando,' recalls Balki. 'After that I didn't watch films for a while. Later, it was at age ten or eleven, when I really started getting interested in films through my friend who lived in the neighbourhood. I was very close to his family and spent almost the entire day with them—eating, sleeping and playing in their house and also went to watch films with them. I started seeing Hindi, Tamil and other regional language films and was gradually introduced to icons like Kamal Haasan, Ilayaraja, Amitabh Bachchan, Rajnikanth, etc. Music was a great pull for me. I can say with certainty that it was actually music that drove me to films. I found it to be a magical experience to hear the music and see a variety of images, quite a lot of which I couldn't comprehend at that time. On one such occasion, I saw an Amitabh Bachchan movie—I think it was *Trishul* and after that I started on my own or occasionally with a friend or two, to watch all Amitabh movies. So while I loved Ilayaraja's music in Tamil movies, the kind of person I always looked upto was Amitabh Bachchan. Bangalore, in a way, was actually a feast for moviegoers. It was truly a cosmopolitan city where one got to see movies in all languages in mainstream theatres. It is the same even today. I learnt Kannada and Telugu through the movies! Though I had studied Hindi in school, nobody used to converse in Hindi in Bangalore. I also learnt all my Hindi mainly because of films.'

As far as learning English goes, Balki gives complete credit to his maternal grandfather, a professor of English Literature, who introduced him to the language very early on in life and made him read voraciously. Every time Balki went to Chennai to meet him, he would be taken to several second hand book shops and handed stacks to read. The grandfather also transferred his fascination for trains onto his grandson! Both would stand for hours at the Central Station in Chennai, and watch trains come and go, keenly observe steam and electric engines, passenger and freight trains, signalling, tracks and so on and so forth. Acknowledges Balki, 'Those trips helped in creating rich images in my mind, which was awesome. Personally, my grandfather has been the biggest influence in my life.'

As it happens with many children, for Balki too, life drifted desultorily between various exams leading upto college. In the midst of the normal routine and schedule of college, cricket and films remained his passions and besides his favourite, Amitabh Bachchan and Rajnikanth films, he also began to watch a lot of western films. Balki remembers having watched at least twenty Fassbinder (acclaimed German film director) films, some of Fellini's (distinguished Italian film director) best works and various other international and Hollywood films, often sitting through all shows at the Blue Diamond on M G Road, which would screen world cinema. Besides movie halls, there was also a video library fellow who introduced him to a lot of films during college. 'I loved films because I always found something more interesting in them than in life around me and imagined that someday I too will make one,' remembers Balki.

And how would that happen? Very presumptuously, this is how he imagined it would—he would be walking in the middle of M G Road in Bangalore and somebody would come with a suitcase carrying a crore of rupees, and would simply ask him to make a film—so convinced was he about his luck! He would often write stories and send it to the Tamil film director, the late Balu Mahendra and others, hoping they will come looking for the great story teller! Ridiculous as it may seem, his fantasy did come true in a way, albeit later in life.

On one listless day, during the fag end of his final year in college, while he was taking a break on the cricket field, Balki saw an advertisement announcing admissions to the Madras Film Institute. When he told his parents about his intention to join the institute, they pressed upon him to reconsider, as no one in the family had anything to do with cinema and also film making courses were not considered formal education those days. But Balki had made up his mind and remembers selling all his books and some other belongings to go to Chennai a few weeks prior to the interview. However, he soon abandoned what was till then an abiding passion and only because the panel of experts at the institute asked him, what he thought were inconsequential questions, about yesteryear actors, directors and in particular, esoteric cinema! So far what Balki had enjoyed were mass entertainers and he thought that if he had to learn the craft from those asking him questions, he may completely lose interest in filmmaking!

With the idea of joining the institute coming to naught, he was at his wit's end when something else caught his attention. The College of Engineering,Guindy affiliated to Anna University, had started a three-year Master of Computer Application (MCA) course that year. Balki signed up for the course but even that turned out to be lacklustre. 'It was so basic and there was so little to do that I hardly attended classes and was again always on the cricket field,' he recalls. As a result, he fell short of attendance and was required to complete the backlog before he could take the final exams. Balki refused to study another few months just to obtain a certificate and walked out of college.

Next, yet another "happy" co-incidence awaited him round the corner in the form of an advertisement by Mudra, asking interested candidates for a course in advertising, to write and send in a hundred words about themselves. Balki knew nothing about advertising, worse, he didn't even realize that it was an advertisement by an ad agency! What attracted him to the advert was the logo of Mudra, which matched the logo that appeared after the credits for *Buniyaad* (one of the most popular television drama series in the mid-Eighties) directed by *Sholay's* director, Ramesh Sippy. Balki sent in the hundred-word autobiographical sketch hoping he may get to work with none other than Ramesh Sippy! A few days later, he was called for an interview where he enthusiastically told the interviewer, Dr Naganand Kumar of Mudra, that he had come to meet Ramesh Sippy. Dr Kumar was astute enough to gauge Balki's potential and after ratifying his can-didature, promised to take him to meet Ramesh Sippy. This was how Balki was baptized into the world of advertising.

'Call it whatever—luck, accident or a happy co-incidence…,'
chuckles Balki.

After the six-month stint at Mudra, Ahmedabad,
Balki was placed in Bangalore and in no time was fascinated
with advertising. To him, advertising was not about selling a
product but a great way of telling stories using the product
as an excuse. He saw how people walked up to an agency
with money and said, please give us an idea, and realized that
this, in a way, was really his dream come true. Adds Balki,
'Of course later you learn to refine the science a little bit and
kind of make the product really the centre of the story. But it
is your story; the product is still an excuse. That's how people
buy products. They want to hear a new, fresh story about
the product. Fortunately, it was my job now! Initially, I had
no idea about it, then I got sucked into it and later literally
blown away by this entire addiction. If you were given a new
problem around which to tell a story every day, you can't get
a bigger addiction than that,' he declares.

Balki stayed with Mudra for the next seven years and
rose to the position of Creative Head for Bangalore and after
some disagreements with the management, shifted to a larger
and iconic agency, Lintas and has stayed with them ever since.
Towards the end of Nineties, he was elevated to the position
of National Creative Director and later became Lintas'
Chairman, a role he has been performing dexterously for the
last over eight years, supported by 750 people across seven
divisions and nine cities, managing more than 250 clients and
helping build India's largest and most successful brands.

Although Balki had reached the pinnacle of his career,
his childhood passion of watching movies continued unabat-
ed and each time a voice in his head would say: 'I'll make one
some day…' That moment finally arrived and Balki narrates
how, 'I was sitting in this very room in 2005, I think, trying to do an advertisement for Lifebuoy soap when suddenly
an idea for Amitji (Amitabh Bachchan) came to me. I had

done a couple of ads with him over the past year for Parker and Dabur, etc. Though I had never spoken to him over the phone, I fortunately had his number from his manager. So I just messaged him saying, I want to meet you, I have an idea. He messaged back, when do you want to meet? I said, anytime you are free? Tomorrow, at 7? He said and I was so zapped and couldn't believe my luck that I had just messaged Amitabh Bachchan and he asked me to see him!

'So I met him and told him the story in two lines. I said, you and Tabu have to do it and if you both aren't in it, this will not be written. Amitji said, just go ahead and write it. I then messaged the same lines to Tabu who was in Los Angeles. She also replied that she loved the idea and on her return, would read the script. As soon as I wrote the complete script, I gave it to Amitji and Tabu. In two days' time I got a call from both saying, let's do it and that's how the movie went into production. It was as simple as that.'

So for you, the actors have to be finalized before the script, I interject.

It is Balki's strong belief that writing is the most fun as well as the most crucial part of filmmaking. 'You put a lot of yourself into writing. I like to say that writing is like a massage-cum-surgery—you think it's beautiful and fantastic but you are actually getting butchered inside! So I always like to sound the idea of a script to actors, who I think suit the roles, and get their sign offs before I go about developing the script. Writing takes too much out of me. And when I am writing for iconic stars, it is necessary that they are excited by the idea as that helps me in crafting their characters,' explains Balki.

How was the feeling of working with your childhood idols, the legendary Amitabh Bachchan and Ilayaraja?

Balki confesses with all earnestness, 'I was lucky that I got to work with someone who is possibly the greatest actor this country has ever seen and who is also the simplest and the most "no fuss" person, which is a very rare combination. The other biggest high for me that followed soon after, was meeting Ilayaraja and P C Sriram. P C was the cinematographer for both *Cheeni Kum* and *Paa*. He has been a dear friend for a long time and yet I am a great fan of his. I had not met Ilayaraja ever. The first time I met him was for my film and I met him more as a fan than a prospective director. Today, I am much closer to him and yet I have never stopped being his fan. I believe I am close to Amitabh Bachchan also and yet I have not stopped being his fan too. I have not become his friend. It's easy to lose your fan feeling in friendship. Friendship brings you closer on a level that a fan can never hope to reach and I would like to be a fan because that is what keeps the awe of cinema going—when you look up, when you aspire, when you have images in your mind and not when you know somebody too well. Both in advertising and in films, you need to have a dream and even if you achieve it, you need to preserve it, because I feel, life becomes very boring if you lose it. Amitabh, Ilayaraja, Lintas – all are institutions for me; they are my dreams that have stayed in my system and therefore still infuse me with the same energy and enthusiasm. I sometimes wonder whether it is my lack of growth or my wish for non-growth. Whatever it is, it certainly is lucky for me,' Balki's analysis seems charming and delightful to me and pretty much the mantra that explains his success and super energetic persona.

I discover how the *idea* of preserving one's dream was handed down to Balki! His father had always wanted to be a lawyer but familial duties had made him take up a job with LIC. Nonetheless, he had kept alive, for a large part of his life, his dream of donning the lawyer's robe. Later at fifty years of age, he acquired a law degree and began practicing as a lawyer soon after retirement!

In today's scenario, no discussion on films can be complete without talking about the "100 crore club". What does Balki think about the current trend of huge marketing push and the much-hyped club becoming the key yardstick for a film's success?

Balki approaches this subject on the basis of fundamentals and opines, 'Marketing is going to pose the biggest danger to films because I believe that people come to the movies to lose themselves into the charming world of celluloid. It is not something that you should thrust on people or deceive them into believing. There have been instances recently when people have come with so much expectation and have been disappointed! You are getting away with it because the films are released in so many theatres. Backed by this marketing hype, you make your money, irrespective of the quality of the film. There are no disincentives to do a bad film! Gone are the days when you said, a good film will work and a bad film will not work. That purity is gone because a bad film can also work, sometimes better than a good film. There are too many people getting away with almost no content and making use of star value to recover their money. That will stop at some point of time. Finally, it's content that will play a bigger role. I hope people become a little smarter and force studios, both large or small, to search for superior content,' he reasons.

The Indian audience today is exposed to the best of world cinema. What will be Bollywood's strength in the face of stiff competition from Hollywood, in terms of technology, special effects or even originality as a lot of Bollywood films are nothing but blatant copies, I want him to comment on this.

'As far as the aspect of rampant copying in Bollywood goes, it cannot be generalized. There is good and bad in every industry. For a lot of people, cinema is business and for several others, it's a great trip. But if the trips don't make money, they tend to die. Obviously therefore, trips must be worthy of making money. It can also be said that even if your trip does not make money, nobody should lose money on your trip and I believe that a good story will never lose money. It goes without saying that we need to tell original stories. It's just that it requires more work and is not as easy as copying. Cinema is a great medium for pushing original ideas. We have the wherewithal and the craft to weave stories in our own unique way and that's what our industry should focus on.

'As far as comparison with Hollywood is concerned, their movies are targeted at an international audience. Hollywood can afford to spend a lot of money in making movies and promoting them worldwide, in discovering technology, grooming people and developing the craft. Our strength however is going to be content and a good story works everywhere. Even there, a *Juno* works, *Bend it Like Beckham* and *Monsoon Wedding* succeed or Ang Lee's previous film, *Brokeback Mountain* moves audiences. These films are not technical masterpieces like a *Life Of Pi* or a *Hobbit* or an *Avatar*. They succeeded purely because of content. Most of Meryl Streep's films are not magnum opuses but they do extremely well and earn 400-500 million dollars, which is huge. Our strength is never going to be technology. India is mainly about content. It will be foolish for us to ape the West. We are a story-telling nation. We don't need to adapt from books, etc. We can generate original stories. India's strength is not about saying how fantastically we execute it. India's strength lies in creating wonderment: Look! What stories we can create! I don't think the world will ever be able to match up to us in that area. In this whole tussle of execution vs. stories, somewhere we are losing track. The fact is that you can learn execution, you can borrow techniques for execution but you will have to bank on telling original stories.

'There is no dearth of original cinema across various languages in India. Today, my fascination is with Marathi cinema, courtesy my wife, Gauri who is a Maharashtrian.

I enjoyed watching *Deool, Tingya, Valu, Masala* etc., but the movie that I found simply earth shattering was, *Gabhricha Paus.* I think it's possibly one of the greatest movies made in this country after *Sadma* (1983) and its original, *Moondram Pirai* in Tamil. These films are as good, if not better than the much celebrated Iranian or any other cinema but it's sad that we as a country don't celebrate these gems. We can certainly do better on that front,' laments Balki.

Don't you think that in view of the recent horrific gang rape in Delhi, Bollywood needs to introspect about raunchy lyrics and lewd picturization of "item songs" in films as well as the stereotypical projection of women in cinema?

Balki reacts, 'The news channels have a far larger role to play in society. Gruesome rapes, murders, and other crime stories seem to be driving several news channels. If we believe that people don't get affected by all that, then logically should they be by some fantastical sequences in films? Censorship, if any, may perhaps be required of news channels—so much gore hits you during prime time! Here lies the dichotomy—the censor board certifies a film 'A' and obviously due to the content, television channels say they will not run an adult film, but most of the programmes on television have adult content. I think that's stupid. Logically, there should be nothing wrong in showing 'A' films on television. Anyway, today everything is freely available on the internet. People should exercise their own discretion. If they reject something, it will not be made. It's how the market dynamics works. Censorship and crying hoarse that some industry is affecting the society is really so silly in the face of all that is happening on television.'

While I agree with Balki that most creative people reject censorship and that television needs introspection and self-regulation, in view of low literacy and economic levels of a vast majority of people in our country, it may be worthwhile that filmmakers exercise discretion as they are by far the largest influencers and seem to fashion opinion when the lights are dimmed in every little village theatre across India.

The female characters in Balki and Gauri's films have certainly been a delight to watch and that's how "use of discretion" by filmmakers comes into play. Currently Balki is working on his next film, once again with his favourite star, Amitabh Bachchan. And as for me who is one amongst those who likes "Balki brand of films", I can't wait to watch another innovative and aesthetic work from the "happy-go-lucky" director.

'Both in advertising and in films, you need to have a dream and even if you achieve it, you need to preserve it. Dreams infuse you with energy and enthusiasm.'

RAKEYSH OMPRAKASH MEHRA

I met Rakeysh after the release of his latest super hit, *Bhaag Milkha Bhaag (BMB)*. He was tied up with its promotions for most of July 2013 and hence we decided to meet in early August. I make it a point to watch *BMB* with my family before the meeting and we unanimously conclude that Rakeysh truly belongs to the masterclass club of film-makers in India.

Rakeysh's office is just a few metres inside Pali village and is built in the style of a duplex cottage. A winding wooden staircase leads up to the aesthetically-designed room of the director, with seating arrangements in the centre, a library and study at one end and his work table on the other. The place exudes a sense of immense peace and serenity.

Rakeysh was born and raised in the walled city of old Delhi (Delhi 100006) with an an older brother and a younger sister. His father worked with the Claridges Hotel in South Delhi and while Rakeysh was still a young boy, the family was required to take residence within the hotel premises. Therefore, from a very early age, Rakeysh was exposed to vastly contrasting environments – the old world charm of *purani Dilli*, and the Claridges which was a throwback to the colonial era of sit down dinners and classy banquets. His parents wanted excellent education for the children, even if it meant going beyond their means, and hence sent Rakeysh and his sister to Air Force Bal Bharti School while the elder one studied at St Columba's.

Rakeysh fared well in academics and excelled in swimming. He first became the captain of his school team, and subsequently participated in inter-zonal swimming championships. Later, as a student of the prestigious Shri Ram College of Commerce(SRCC), he represented Delhi University and made it to the qualifying rounds of Asian Games in 1982.

'I had no plans to join the film industry. I am here because I followed my instincts. I don't know where this will lead to, whether I am meant to be here or will move on to something else. But while I am here, I am thoroughly enjoying telling stories through movies. I feel very strongly about the movies. They give me an opportunity to express myself. It's like a canvas where you paint your emotions and connect with people. For me, cinema is a personal journey which has no final destination. This is life for me, this is what I do and it's very difficult for me to treat it strictly as a profession. The lines are totally blurred for me,' expresses Rakeysh as he narrates how films came about for him.

On completing his graduation, Rakeysh started off with Eureka Forbes in their sales team. Within a few months, he broke the national sales record and paradoxically also lost interest in sales. Next, he set up a garment exports business in partnership with a friend from SRCC and grew it rapidly to a few hundred machines and *karigars* (artisans), operating out of a couple of factories. After spending nearly a year and a half in the venture, an opportunity in the field of advertising opened up for Rakeysh through a chance interaction at a dinner party. Rakeysh decided to take up the offer, and left the garment business to his friend who is a leading exporter today.

During his early years in advertising, a Chandigarh-based automobile company, Swaraj Mazda, manufacturers of Light Commercial Vehicles (LCVs) happened to be one of Rakeysh's clients. As the firm was in technical collaboration with Mazda Motor Corporation, Japan, Rakeysh was deputed for a short stint to Hiroshima to not only understand the product, but also the Japanese work ethics of discipline, punctuality, etc. 'The exercise was meant to "Japanesefy" me,' chuckles Rakeysh and in retrospect feels it was a memorable experience in his career.

However, the turning point in his life came about when he moved to a bigger agency, Ulka where amongst several others, he met the leading ad film director, Prahlad Kakkar of Genesis Film Productions, who happened to be in Delhi to direct the adverts for Hero Honda. Unforunately, just before the shoots were to commence, Kakkar met with a serious accident and was confined to bed with a dislocated shoulder and one man's misery proved to be another man's opportunity. As the representative of the agency, Rakeysh was aware that if the shoots got delayed, Ulka ran the risk of losing a prestigious client and hence took it upon himself to shoot the films under Prahlad's guidance. Prahlad was very impressed with Rakeysh's *debut* at filmmaking and told him on his way back to Mumbai, 'You don't belong here, you belong to Bombay.'

Rakeysh took Prahlad's cue and quit his job at Ulka, despite offers of a substantial salary increase, a house and car and decided to move to Mumbai which was indisputably the Mecca for advertising. When he shared his plans with his parents, who at that point were thinking of finding a suitable match for him since he was settled in his career, they told him, '*Jo tujhe sahi lagta hai, tu kar* (Do what you think is right). But hope you understand that it's not going to be easy. Go with your eyes open.'

With a single assignment in hand, gifted to him as a farewell present by his boss in Ulka, Rakeysh landed in Mumbai at Prahlad's doorstep, 'Here I am, you had told me so!' Indeed, Prahlad had shown him the Bombay Dream and it fell upon him to support it, which he did with all the grace possible! Rakeysh launched the Flicks Motion Picture Company and started operating his "office" from the space provided by Prahlad near the staircase outside his office on the 6th floor. 'I would run up and down to attend phone calls,' remembers Rakeysh about how his makeshift office functioned in the initial years. It was also at Prahlad's office where he met his future wife, Bharathi, who still continues to edit all his films.

Slowly but surely, Rakeysh found his footing in Mumbai. After a period of about five years of dedicated work, he was recognized as a talented ad filmmaker and by the mid-Nineties, his company ranked amongst the top three in India. It may be recalled that the first ever brand endorsed by Amitabh Bachchan for BPL was shot by Rakeysh. 'From there began a student-mentor kind of relationship with Amitabh Bachchan. A sustained period of professional and personal interactions with him (including directing the music video album, *Aby Baby* of *Eer Bir Phatte* fame) led to the making of my first feature film, *Aks* in 2001, which was a paranormal thriller,' shares Rakeysh. Though *Aks* did not fare well at the box office, it was received well by critics and bagged the Filmfare Best Actor award for Amitabh Bachchan. Critical appreciation alone however was not good enough, either for Amitabh Bachchan or Rakeysh. While Amitabh was struggling to save his Juhu bungalow, Prateeksha and other properties in Delhi from being attached by debtors after the debacle of his entrepreneurial venture, ABCL, Rakeysh was also laden with large debts and had put out his residential bungalow in Pali hill as a collateral. He had not only invested all his savings, but also borrowed both from Citibank and the open market at a steep interest rate to make *Aks*, but the film had failed to recover the money. Rakeysh was left with no choice but to get back to shooting ad films and it finally took him four years to get his bungalow free of lien.

'I have never understood the idea of hoarding wealth. I only know how to create wealth and live for the moment. I like buying property but I won't flinch even for a moment if the need arises to liquidate it to be able to do the work I enjoy doing in my present,' he opines.

Although *Aks* had happened on an impulse, it gave Rakeysh the conviction that movies is what he enjoyed doing the most; all he ever wanted to do was this! So while he tried to repair his financial status by getting back to ad filmmaking, the elusive film script weighed heavily on his mind. Rakeysh was supremely conscious of the fact that he had neither studied in any film school nor assisted anybody and had blindly taken the plunge. The lack of formal knowledge hit him deeply and he completely submitted himself to the art of filmmaking. He also noticed that western films were technically far superior in finesse and made it a point that during his travels to London on work, which he often did, he would overstretch his budgets and stay to hone the technique of filmmaking. And it was during one of these trips that he stumbled upon the works of greats such as Akira Kurusawa and Federico Fellini. He watched their films intently, read about them extensively and came to the conclusion that in order to create original work, deep introspection was of critical importance—to hear the inner voice which arises from one's life experiences, understand what you want to say to the world and then give it cinematic expression. 'To be able to hear your own voice and discover originality for the sake of art, it becomes imperative to shut out the din of people's voices around you…. For me it is very important that the story is either born out of your own crisis or arises when somewhere deep down you can relate to someone else's crisis—the protagonist's crisis—so that you become one with it and can tell the story more personally and sincerely,' he says spelling out the method that works for him.

Thus came about *Rang De Basanti (RDB)* in 2006. The film was inspired by the environment Rakeysh had witnessed – the early Eighties when he was studying in SRCC—when India was just emerging from one of its darkest political phases in the aftermath of the Emergency imposed in June 1975. 'At Delhi University, the atmosphere was highly charged and every youngster was infused with a deep desire to bring about change, stamp out corruption and bring in revolution,' he remembers. Later, after he graduated from college, the pro-democracy Tiananmen Square protests in China made headlines and stirred similar emotions in India as well. Not long after, the discontent with the establishment echoed in India in the form of the Mandal Commission protests by students. Rakeysh witnessed this movement at close quarters and also the government's attempt to quell it by using force against students. Several such influences over the years—like watching a documentary on NDTV on MIG crashes, the model of a plane placed in his school compound, the tricolour unfurled on Independence or Republic Day, the parades he watched in Delhi – finally found expression in *Rang De Basanti.* 'Direction is about being in touch with yourself,' Rakeysh reiterates the point and mentions how the characters of the five young men in the film were based on his friends in college. The film was considered a landmark as it appealed both to the critics and masses and won Rakeysh the Best Director Award at the 2006 Filmfare Awards, the National Film Award and also a BAFTA nomination for the Best Foreign Language Film.

Continuing with his conviction of movies growing out of one's consciousness, Rakeysh began preparing for his next film, *Delhi-6* based on his close understanding of the Walled City where he was born. So while *RDB* was about the young men's commitment to the nation and the transformation thereof, *Delhi-6* was an insight into the area's complex and delicate social fabric in the backdrop of religion.

'Although Hindu-Muslim *mohallas* co-existed and celebrated Diwali and Eid together, it all seemed superficial. The undercurrents of fear and uncertainty always remained and the smallest incidents had the potential to disturb the fragile calm. I would often wonder that despite living in the same neighbourhood and intermingling with each other, one never heard of any romances or inter-caste marriages! The sense of India converging was really on a very superficial level. I have never really understood who Allah is or who is Bhagwan and why should people fight over religion. That's what I showed in *Delhi-6* and perhaps raised some uncomfortable questions,' he explains.

Even though *Delhi-6* didn't win at the box office, it was noticed and praised for its originality, innovative style, cinematography and earthiness and was selected for the prestigious Venice Film Festival. It was termed as "(Un) Bollywood" by *Variety*, a reputed and popular American entertainment trade magazine, and went on to win two national awards as well.

Rakeysh's latest film, *Bhaag Milkha Bhaag*, a biopic on India's most revered athlete, Milkha Singh, is yet another extension of his beliefs and reflects that while it's futile to control the circumstances prevailing upon you, you can control the manner in which you respond to them. The film showcases "Flying Sikh" aka Milkha Singh's dramatic life, a twelve-year-old who witnesses the gruesome massacre of his family during Partition, his unending struggle to survive and finally emerging as an iconic athlete.

Rakeysh was primarily drawn to *BMB* due to his disillusionment with Partition and his deep conviction in the invincibility of the human spirit. About the time when Rakeysh was completing his graduation, his family had shifted out of the Claridges to the Lajpat Nagar area in South Delhi which was largely a refugee resettlement colony built on the shared pain and anguish of people who had crossed over from Pakistan in 1947. Although Rakeysh had heard stories of horror and massacres of the Partition era ad nauseum, it was in 1984 during the Sikh riots that he actually witnessed the extreme pain and fear of a community. But Rakeysh was familiar with the legend of Milkha Singh even before that and it was during his swimming practice sessions at the National Stadium in Delhi, when his coaches and fellow sportspersons would often narrate anecdotes about how Milkha would faint during practice, but show extraordinary resilience by getting back to the tracks; and how he would fill up a bucket with his sweat after a work out, etc. Later in an autobiographical account of Milkha Singh written in Gurumukhi, Rakeysh came across the details of his early life, the extremely bitter and painful experience of Partition and a lost and abused childhood. It was this part of his life, more than how the world viewed Milkha Singh, that made the story special for Rakeysh and gave him a "compulsive" impetus to make the film.

Sharing his views on Partition, Rakeysh feels that compared to the West, the subcontinent has somehow failed to handle its historical divisions and tragedies. For instance, the horrific Nazi concentration camps, Jewish ghettos and mass exterminations during the Second World War by Germans are kept alive albeit only as part of history by a group of nations who have succeeded in putting their dark past behind and moved forward to function as an economic conglomerate! Why can't India and Pakistan resolve to thrive as a unified region in the geopolitical space, he questions?

After what turned out to be an intensely passionate discussion, we shift focus to his future projects, and the shooting of his romantic film, titled *Mirza Sahiban* in 2014. 'I tend to romanticize everything, even a cup of coffee!' he comments and I wonder how someone like him will interpret the theme of timeless love. While he reveals his idea behind his next project, I am taken aback by its title: *Casual Kamasutra!* But regain my composure when I hear a lovely story about the struggles and eventual victory of a young man from rural India who pledges to take on giant retail outlets modeled on western markets with his brand, "Casual Kamasutra". I also gather how Rakeysh was inspired to tell this story after his encounters with several *karigars* in India's hinterland and his fascination with the abounding wealth of art, music, and culture in towns like Madhubani, Benaras, Chanderi, Khajuraho, etc.

Almost sounding like the protagonist from *Casual Kamasutra*, he says, 'We can make the best films in the world and should demand respect from the world. The idea is not to chase the Oscars but to take our stories to the world. *Hamare paas aisi kahaniyan hain* (We are in possession of such stories). We can put India on the global map with our movies. If Ratan Tata and Narayana Murthy can do it, why can't we, what's the big deal?' he exhorts. 'What we need is deep introspection and realization that we are in the business for excellence; a new model has to emerge where the commerce follows the passion and not the other way round. Filmmakers and artists shouldn't think like stockbrokers or bankers. I can't understand the concept of a hit weekend or the latest race for being in the 100 crore club. Films are artworks and should be part of a nation's history and should continue to make money long after one is dead and gone, not just a

100 crores but 1,000 crores! Fortunately, new media – DVDs, the internet – will be able to do that; perpetuity makes more business sense to me than monitoring weekend figures,' he says expressing his disgruntlement with the current trend of "crores" becoming the focal point for cinema.

He adds, 'Also why do we need to make the largest number of movies in the world, why can't we change the focus to making a few but the finest movies in the world? I can't understand our obsession with numbers! For being recognized on an international level, change has to happen. Art needs to grow organically instead of being a shoddy copy or remake of something that has been created in the West or in China or elsewhere.'

Emphasizing on the importance of keeping originality sacrosanct to the art of filmmaking, he says, 'We have to perhaps begin by undoing the Bollywood nomenclature. I don't understand the term Bollywood; I don't know where Bollywood is. There is no hill here like Hollywood which has a sign saying HOLLYWOOD! So Bollywood is at best a bastardized term, more for the West to identify this market. It suits them to call it by a name which is colloquially easy on their tongues! I don't see any reason why we have to ratify that! As far as I am concerned, I don't identify with Bollywood at all.

'Let's not forget that these are exciting times when the world has opened its gates for us. Besides the traditional overseas markets like the US, UK and East Africa, new markets like Australia, Japan, South America, the Middle East, Central and Eastern Europe are also showing encouraging trends. Globalization, as I understand, is when you can tell an "Indian" story to the outside world, when the world buys your product willingly and large numbers consume it globally. For instance, the way Asterix comics, Korean films and Japanese anime are devoured. If the Japanese and the Koreans can do it, why can't Indians make their mark? You don't want to be a B-grade presence in international festivals. That is derivative art which doesn't automatically make you global. What makes you global is when you appropriate a place in the popular psyche and that happens by being original, like the films of Fellini and Kurusawa which are purely Italian and Japanese stories and yet have a worldwide appeal.'

He further focuses on how that kind of specialized creativity can be achieved, and says, 'It can only blossom when you are in touch with yourself and the inner self is nurtured by calm surroundings; inspiration counts for just 1% of creativity, 99% of it is perseverance and practice. There's so much truth in the old adage of "practice makes a man perfect". There are innumerable examples of such masters around us. For example, Gulzar who began in the early Sixties and since then has been consistently devoted to his writing, producing great work not just in films but also children's books and in other non-commercial spheres. A R Rahman, Aamir Khan, Ronnie Screwvala, Binod Pradhan, I count all of them amongst the game changers of Hindi cinema due to their sheer grit and dedication. Look at Aamir who is a path breaker for choosing to do only one film at a time when his contemporaries were doing as many as nineteen films together. I appreciate Farhan Akhtar for approaching his role in *Bhaag Milkha Bhaag* as a character and not as a hero, and each time you look at him, you see the character of Milkha Singh and forget the persona of the star. I admire Binod Pradhan's dedication to his craft, his excellence as a cinematographer. That extra stroke of genius becomes evident only after you give up your ego; submit yourself completely and connect with your cosmic energy; shut out the noise of the world that gives you pre-conceived notions; get consumed by your passion without employing any cushioning or manipulation; feel your instinct. We should strive to maintain the high standards and keep the purity alive in cinema and not settle for mediocrity. That's being shortsighted and shouldn't be allowed to happen,' cautions Rakeysh.

A city that once realized his dreams has today, rues Rakeysh, become unbearable. 'I don't see a very interesting future for this city as the film capital. It is no longer the city of dreams. It's become a city to leave and not one to come to. The infrastructure is crumbling, studios have been razed to the ground, and Mumbai is now simply unaffordable! How can we expect talent and artists from smaller towns, those who may have wonderful new stories to tell, to come to this city to make it in cinema? On another note, earlier when people like Dharmendra and Dilip Kumar came to this city, they would apparently catch their breath by spending a few hours at Juhu beach. Today, Juhu beach stinks and suffocates.

'Who is nurturing the city, making sure that transport and public welfare get proper focus? A city that can be judged as top class is one that takes care of its children and old people. Today Mumbai has become a black hole and one wonders what kind of art will come out of a city like this? I have been to movie capitals of the world which are thriving and vibrant cities like, Los Angeles, Paris, Tokyo, New York, London and Amsterdam, where painting, music, dance and sports co-exist and find equal exuberance. That's the kind of evolving cultural vibrance and dynamism that is needed for films to thrive. Cinema can't thrive in isolation and mass produced out of corporate offices,' he sounds a grim warning but at the same time does not want to give in to helplessness. He believes that change can be brought about by his contemporaries by creating better space—say between Mumbai and Pune or Nasik where there isn't so much pressure on land—and make that a centre for cinema to grow. 'Where newcomers can take a place on rental for a sum of 2,000 rupees and not pay hefty sums of 15,000 for a paying guest accommodation and scrounge for monies to shoot portfolios!' he says.

In view of the recent spate of horrific crimes against women, I want to know his views on the current trend of the "imperative" item numbers in cinema. Would he ever have one in his films? Rakeysh responds firmly, 'I am very clear and have no confusion on the issue that item songs are totally avoidable! To say that it's the need of a script is only subterfuge—disguising something that's unacceptable. There were times when people said Sati, dowry deaths, child marriage etc., *hota hai, chalta aa raha hai* (happens and are part of a long tradition), but that doesn't make what's wrong, right. Shoddiness should not be confused with entertainment.'

As a concluding remark, I prod Rakeysh to say something for those who may dream of being part of the world of films. Offering the crux of his long and successful years in cinema, he says, 'The only advice I can give is if they are aspiring to be directors, they should have something to say or as cinematographers they should have some pictures to show. If not, then it's a sheer waste of time and money. The expression has to be personal to an individual, coupled with a compelling desire to share it with the world. Finally it does not matter whether one has gone to a film school or not, has a support system or not. Eventually, the instinct and perseverance will reign supreme.'

What I liked about Rakeysh is his intense sensitivity and uncompromising standards, and I am convinced that one day, he may just break out and shine on world stage….

'A new model has to emerge where the commerce follows the passion and not the other way round. Filmmakers and artists shouldn't think like stockbrokers or bankers. I can't understand the concept of a hit weekend or the latest race for being in the 100 crore club. Films are artworks and should be part of a nation's history.'

THE MIDAS TOUCH

ROHIT SHETTY

Mumbai, the city of dreams has been incredibly generous to innumerable people. Starting from a bare scratch, these individuals have gone on to earn tremendous name, fame and wealth through their talent, sheer resilience and above all good fortune which they themselves are quick to acknowledge. Rohit Shetty is one such person who has been blessed with phenomenal success in this city. He is the only director who has the rare distinction of having delivered seven consecutive hits of which six are in the coveted "100 crore club" and his latest, *Chennai Express* crossing the threshold to make it to 200 crores!

In early August 2013, a month and a half before the release of *Chennai Express,* I meet Rohit at his sprawling new office on New Link road in Andheri West. Spread over an area of more than 5,000 square feet, one half of this expansive space houses the director's office, the sleek production and editing offices, a lounge for guests and a well serviced café. The other comprises a partially covered large terrace with an air hockey table and a basket ball net fitted on the wall. I am told that Shah Rukh Khan prefers the terrace compared to the comfortable lounge area inside.

It's a Sunday and Rohit is casually dressed in shorts and a T-shirt which stylishly shows off his tattooed biceps. A French window runs through the entire width of his room and on his desk sit framed pictures of his son and father and several trophies and awards beside a large screen placed on a swivel. An entire ledge behind his desk displays a variety of car models and apparently belong to his son who shares Rohit's passion for the "fast and the furious"!

Born to action director-turned-actor of the Sixties and Seventies, M B Shetty, famous for his menacing roles as a villain, Rohit's love for action is almost like an inheritance. His mother was also a stunt artist and that's how his parents had met on a film set. Rohit lost his father at the age of eight and his mother was forced to rejoin the industry as a junior artist to support a large family that besides Rohit, included his four sisters. By the time Rohit turned fifteen, he had made up his mind to drop out of school and start working as he could see that his mother was struggling to make ends meet and felt awkward to ask her for money.

For as long as he remembers, all he ever wanted to do was to be an action director like his father and make films. Even as he seriously began to scout for work, one of his sisters introduced him to director Kuku Kohli, who was directing Ajay Devgn in his debut lead role in *Phool Aur Kaante*. However it was a disappointing first meeting as Kuku politely declined to hire Rohit saying that he already had enough assistants and couldn't afford to take on more, but asked the young man to stay in touch.

And from then on began a gruelling routine which lasted for eighteen long months: Rohit would devotedly go to meet Kuku Kohli everyday either at his house or on the sets or elsewhere just to mark his presence and return home. 'The period tested my patience. All my friends were going to college and here I was sitting at home. There were too many questions and the mind wavered a lot. However, at that age one was also extremely innocent; I had more faith than frustration in the way life was treating me. I kept the hope alive and didn't change track.'

In 1992, Rohit finally got a break with Kuku Kohli as an assistant director for *Ek Aur Kohinoor* (interestingly, Abhishek Kapoor, the director of *Rock On* and *Kai Po Che* was signed as the hero for the film). However, the film had to be stalled after shooting eight reels due to some controversy and eventually, never got made. Kuku later went on to make *Suhaag* in 1994 and repeated Ajay Devgn in the lead role and through the first half of the Nineties, Rohit assisted Kohli on nearly five films and learnt the ropes of filmmaking.

And then in 1996, Ajay Devgn started his production company, eponymously called, Devgan Films, and asked Rohit to join the venture. 'When I look back, it was that one call by Ajay that changed my life. I can say conclusively that the first brick for my successful career was laid by him,' acknowledges Rohit. Devgan Films released their first film, *Pyaar Toh Hona Hi Tha* in 1998 with Ajay and Kajol in the lead for which Rohit was roped in as associate director. This was followed by *Hindustan Ki Kasam* (1999), directed by Ajay's father, Veeru Devgan and then *Raju Chacha* (2000) directed by his cousin, Anil Devgan. It was during the filming of *Raju Chacha*, when as a token of appreciation, Ajay promised Rohit that he would get to direct the company's next film. However, as luck would have it, *Raju Chacha* sank at the box office and Devgan Films suffered huge losses. But Ajay stuck by his commitment and made sure that even if his next film was not his home production—*Zameen* with Abhishek Bachchan and Bipasha Basu—Rohit would direct it.

'So it was all planned. I didn't have to struggle for my script. Before finally getting to direct a film, I had worked for eleven years as an assistant director. It was a slow and gradual process after which Ajay decided that it was time for me to direct a film for him. There are many such instances in the industry where associate directors have gone on to become successful directors. I think this is the only industry where a big opportunity is laid out for you! Look at Karan Johar, he has mentored so many directors. One of my assistants, Ashish R Mohan went on to make *Khiladi 786* with Akshay Kumar. Another one, Rajeev is working on a script. It's like a cycle. You work for 7-8 years as an assistant and then you write your own scripts and direct your movies. I feel good when my assistant directors go on to become full-fledged directors. It feels great when they discuss their scripts with me; I even shot a few sequences of *Khiladi 786* for Ashish. My ADs are like family to me. Compared to when I started, the whole scenario has changed today and I think people who are making films now are very lucky. Everything is more professional now and there is a lot of work; more films are being made and then there is television too. It's possible to make your film in a relatively short span of time unlike the long struggle of earlier days and there is a lot of recognition for your talent as well because of the wide media network,' reflects Rohit.

Unfortunately, Rohit's directorial debut, *Zameen* bombed at the box office but the industry refused to write him off as yet. The reason amongst several others, was his past association with people, which had earned Rohit enough credibility and goodwill and this was proven when he was offered to direct a thriller for Ashtavinayak Cine Vision in the aftermath of *Zameen's* debacle. It was also during this time when his close friend and actor-director, Neeraj Vora of *Phir*

Hera Pheri fame, narrated a story to him based on the well known Gujarati comic play, *Ghar Ghar,* and thus was born the *Golmaal* franchise in 2006 with sequels, *Golmaal Returns* and *Golmaal 3* in 2008 and 2010 respectively.

Rohit Shetty has been on a roll ever since and has the rare distinction of delivering seven consecutive hits including, *All The Best: Fun Begins* (2009); *Singham* (2011); *Bol Bachchan* (2012) and the latest, *Chennai Express* in 2013.

After the tremendous success of *Golmaal 3,* Shah Rukh Khan approached Rohit to make a movie with him. In what can only be termed as a wonderful coincidence, it was as if Rohit had a tailormade role for the superstar. Interestingly, sometime in 2008, K Subhash, a Tamil director, had narrated a love story with an unusual, whacky kind of tangent, to Rohit. It was about a man from Mumbai who travels to Rameshwaram and falls in love during the journey…the story that finally got made as *Chennai Express!*

Rohit's association with Shah Rukh triggered off speculation in the industry that all wasn't well between the director and his one-time mentor, Ajay Devgn. Rohit laughs off the conjecture and says, 'If I have a great relationship with Ajay and Shah Rukh wants to do a film with me because he appreciates the films I have made, that's no reason for my relationship with Ajay to go sour! If you are growing and ex-panding your work, there is no reason why your old relation-ships should get strained. I have done *Chennai Express* with Shah Rukh and I am doing my next, *Singham 2* with Ajay. After signing Shah Rukh, Ajay and I did *Singham 1* and *Bol Bachchan* together. So all this talk about strained relationship is only a figment of people's imagination,' he says dismissing all misgivings.

Chennai Express, co-produced by Shah Rukh Khan's production company, Red Chillies Entertainment and UTV will go down in history as one of the most expensive movies made in 2013. I want Rohit to comment about the current trend of co-productions and an increasing preference for corporate studios as partners over individual financiers.

Justifying the phenomenon, Rohit says, 'Making films costs a lot of money these days. No solo producer can afford to take individual risks and stake big monies on a film's success. Usually a few producers get together and pool in resources to make a big budget film. In the earlier days, neither were the budgets high, nor the approach to filmmaking as professional,' he comments. Amongst the various corporate houses that produce films, Rohit thinks that Ronnie Screwvala and Siddharth Roy Kapur of UTV possess strong conviction, a very good understanding of the business, and a sound gut feel of what clicks with the audiences.

Elaborating further on the effect of corporate studios, he says, 'Corporatization of cinema has been a boon for filmmakers. It has undoubtedly created a healthy environment in the industry, and as a result several new directors are now able to raise funds for bold and novel story ideas. Each one of us is creating our own distinct brand of cinema. We are happy and secure in our space and have genuine respect for our fellow directors. When we meet on social occasions or on some television shows and even sometimes when we walk the ramp together (chuckles!), we chat for hours and learn from each other.

'Very often, being associated with the same corporate house strengthens the feeling of camaraderie amongst us and results in a wonderful domino effect. For example, if *Yeh Jawani Hai Diwani* or *Barfi,* produced by UTV, does well, it helps me in *Chennai Express* where UTV can pump in the profits made in their earlier ventures. If *3 Idiots* produced by Reliance did well, it helped me in the making of *Singham* and *Singham's* success helped *Talaash* which was co-produced by Reliance,' Rohit explains the dynamics.

Rohit's cordial approach towards his fellow directors also emanates from the way he visualizes the bigger picture,

'There are 200-265 films made in a year. Let's presume that even if a director works round the clock, he can only manage to make a single film or at best, finish scripting and pre-production of one more? That's what I am currently doing and am happy. Where is the competition? I feel blessed that I have so much work. It's not as if I don't want to compete! But only with myself; to do better work than what I have done earlier.' Despite his extraordinary success, he says humbly, 'I am still a student and constantly learning from my environment. There is a lot you can learn from people around you. For instance, when I look at Ajay Devgn, I notice that despite several years and fabulous hits in the industry, he is still as nervous, anxious, and rehearses dedicatedly as he did for his earlier films. He still retains the traits of a newcomer and gives his best.

'After having worked with Shah Rukh Khan on *Chennai Express* recently, I observed that besides his enormous talent, his innate goodness makes him a true superstar. He is extremely humble; the respect he gives me, he also gives to the spot boy on a set. Even after so many years in the industry and most importantly, being on top of the heap, he is completely a director's actor and works like a newcomer. Let's not forget that he comes with great experience but he listens patiently and believes in a no-nonsense approach once he is on the set. Unlike the clichéd image of a Bollywood star surrounded by his entourage, SRK doesn't even carry a phone when he is on the set. He is the simplest actor and human being to work with. That's what makes him a superstar and that's why he retains the top position! That's as much true for some other stars as well like Salman, Akshay or Aamir. They are undoubtedly special people. Imagine, to be able to retain the charisma for close to two decades!' opines Rohit.

Drawing from his own experience of nearly two decades and that of several others who have witnessed tremendous success, Rohit believes that a formal training in filmmaking is not mandatory for success and states how film institutes have become obsolete and need an urgent overhaul. 'Most often, people who teach cinema have either not made a film in years or in some cases, have not made a film at all. So how can they teach?' he questions. Elaborating on this anomaly, he says that there is a tendency amongst film institutes to *intimidate* students by giving them examples of great directors like Guru Dutt, Bimal Roy or Satyajit Ray. 'They were legends. The institutes teach you how *Pyasa* was made and students come out wanting to be Guru Dutt! How can a new kid be expected to reach that level? Allow him to create his own identity. Filmmaking is not rocket science and nor are we engaged in making a nuclear bomb! We are here to entertain people. Also students come out of film schools with a mindset that people working in commercial films are stupid which is a completely wrong notion. The entire methodology of teaching cinema in our country is severely flawed. I have seen films made by one or two film institutes and they were mediocre! They were not only technically flawed, out of focus shots being the worse, they used the same, tedious 60s' lines! I think it's time students are encouraged to make their kind of cinema,' he professes.

Talking of which, Rohit is of the firm belief that one of the reasons for his "consecutive hits" is his fantastic team including some members who are still in their late teens! He demands a professional, no-nonsense approach to work from them and at the same time ensures that they enjoy working and have a happy and high energy atmosphere on the set. For the first one year, he doesn't particularly "teach", but keeps a close watch and gauges their interest. 'Luckily all the people who have come to me have been very enthusi-astic to learn and that's the kind of passion I look for in an individual. If that's in surfeit, I feel all else can be taught! If you ask me, I'll say with conviction that I have never been to *work* in the last twenty-two years. That's because I enjoy doing what I do. There hasn't been a single day when I didn't want to go to office or shoot,' says Rohit.

Sharing another key factor for success, he says, 'Besides a passion for work, the other important factor in film-making is to be your own person and not be like someone else. There are many directors who failed because they wanted to be like Yash Chopra or Karan Johar. Simply put, if you make up your mind that you can't please everybody all the time, you'll be the happiest person. There is an audience for every kind of film. My films for example, cater to a family audience. Some people love them and some don't—it's a product, you can't appease every consumer! When I travel around the country, kids, women, and men of all ages come up to me at airports and malls to tell me that they like my films. I cater to that particular set of audience and the day they stop loving what I show, I will think of making something else. Till then I will stick to what I do and will try to make my movies grander and better,' he declares.

Commenting on the exclusive "100 crore club", of which he is an illustrious member, Rohit feels that very soon the notion will be passé and become the "new normal" for films. With equal aplomb, he also demolishes the latest trend of creating marketing blitzkrieg for films and says, 'It's true that we have long promotions. We *prepare* our audiences and put them in a habit for our forthcoming release. They see us in a few advertisements, on a few channels, in some four songs, etc. Whether this creates a difference or not, we haven't yet figured out. The industry doesn't have a commom view on how much promotion should be done. I am totally against this trend as we end up spending around 15-18 crores on promotion and publicity and in order to recover that amount, the film is expected to do business worth thirty-six crores, almost double of the original spends because 50% of our revenue is taken away by the government! The huge publicity budget is unnecessary pressure on a director. I am totally in favour of cutting down the publicity budgets because it's almost like making a separate film. It's also extremely boring as I am expected to say favourable things about an unreleased film ad nauseum! Directing a film is serious business, there's lots to do once the shooting is over like, post-production, editing, re-recording and much else. On top of that, you are expected to take time out for promotions.

'We need to figure out a way whereby we can cut down the budgets and the duration of publicity. The producers and directors associations have had meetings on this issue, but nothing has come to fruition. We can perhaps learn from South Indian films which are promoted for a stipulated period of thirty days and follow a strict rule whereby a producer can only advertise four times before the release of a film and in a certain specified format,' Rohit emphatically expresses his views on the subject. Further, he truly believes that showbiz is one of the most honest businesses in the world. One can't bribe, lure or threaten the audience with pre-release gimmickry or PR gigs; it's finally the film's merit which makes it a winner.

I couldn't help but ask him about critics and one of their deep obsessions to constantly apply the Hollywood yardstick to Hindi films and he responds, 'If you see from a business point of view, we are totally different from Hollywood. You just can't compare the two for the simple reason that our market is much smaller than Hollywood and hence our budgets are also tinier. Hollywood makes films in a single language which is English, and caters to the whole of America and the world. Hindi films don't even cater to the whole of India! Besides Hindi, films are also made in Tamil, Telugu, Gujarati, Punjabi, Kannada, Malayalam, etc. A film that does well in Mumbai may not do the same business in Tamil Nadu because the State has its own dynamics. Today we are almost at par with Hollywood in terms of state-of-the-art equipment, trained technicians and for that matter, even talent. For example, in the past, Hollywood outsourced the special effects for films like the *Gladiator, Fast and Furious*, to India. So technical expertise is not the issue. The point is that we don't have the kind of budgets Hollywood commands because of the size of its market. If a budget of 1,300-1,400 crores is made available to a good director here, I am sure he can also make movies like *Transformers*. Further, assuming that such budgets become feasible, how shall we then go about recovering the costs from a Hindi film?' he voices his skepticism.

Going forward, while Rohit wants to constantly challenge himself to make larger-than-life films, he also acknowledges the fact that he is grateful for what he has achieved so far. 'I started from nowhere and today I am blessed to have so many people working with me. There are many great and talented directors who have not achieved the success they deserve. I must be the luckiest man on this earth to have enough work and to be working with superstars like Shah Rukh and Ajay. I believe I should be happy with what I have and try to make as many people happy.' He continues to be in the philosophical vein and sums up our meeting by saying, 'We (filmmakers) are neither bad nor good. We are just like normal people who go about their work, have chosen a livelihood, follow our passion and are fortunate to be in a field where we can entertain and make more and more people happy.'

Now, this is definitely a noble intention that should go miles!

'We don't have the kind of budgets Hollywood commands because of the size of its market. If a budget of 1,300-1,400 crores is made available to a good director here, we can also make movies like *Transformers*.'

SUDHIR MISHRA

Sudhir Mishra is acknowledged as one of the leading lights of the new wave, parallel or arthouse cinema movement of the Eighties to which his earliest award-winning films like, *Yeh Woh Manzil Toh Nahin, Main Zinda Hoon* and *Dharavi* belong. His other and more recent works include the critically acclaimed, *Hazaaron Khwahishen Aisi, Khoya Khoya Chand, Chameli, Yeh Saali Zindagi* and the latest *Inkaar* which was released in January 2013 starring Chitrangada Singh and Arjun Rampal.

I wonder what is it like for a filmmaker to straddle vastly different eras and manage the transition from arthouse genre of the Eighties to mainstream cinema of contemporary times with such finesse. To understand the versatile director Sudhir Mishra's journey, on this fine afternoon in September, I am on my way to his office located at Aaram Nagar in Versova, Andheri West, reckoned as one of Mumbai's creative hubs.

Off Versova's main road, the lane turns further right towards a small, open parking space of Aaram Nagar 2. A few cottages line up the L-shaped expanse opposite the parking lot and at the far end of the curve is Sudhir Mishra's cottage; the ground floor is where his parents live and the compact mezzanine floor is his office, divided between his cabin and work stations for his team members. His work desk is in the centre of the cabin and flanking it are pictures of a young Sudhir Mishra receiving the National Award from the late President Giani Zail Singh for his debut film, *Yeh Woh Manzil Toh Nahin,* in 1988. Another picture shows him receiving the prestigious Ordre des Arts et des Lettres by the French Government (equivalent to a knighthood). Also on the same wall are pictures of his late wife and eminent film editor, Renu Saluja and brother, Sudhanshu Mishra.

Appreciation for the fine arts, literature and films was an integral part of Sudhir's childhood. His maternal grandfather, Dwarka Prasad Mishra, besides being a freedom fighter and later Chief Minister of Madhya Pradesh, was also a prolific author. On the other side, Sudhir's father, Devendra Nath Mishra was a brilliant mathematician and a Doctor of Science (D.Sc.) from Paris, who chose to be a university professor. Their large joint family in Lucknow would often get together in the sprawling *aangan* (verandah) of their family home to watch films on a projector, and little Sudhir would find a place in the lap of either his father or one of his uncles. Later, Sudhir's father along with a few other aficionadoes even went on to set up the Lucknow Film Society.

The earliest memories that Sudhir has are of his paternal great-grandfather, Jai Narain Mishra who had an extraordinary life—from a door-to-door seller of blankets, he became an extremely successful businessman and was later conferred with the title of Rai Sahib by the British. Jai Narain's large joint family (his daughter and five grandsons including Sudhir's father) was not only educated, liberal and firmly agnostic, it was also singularly matriarchal and the Mishra women were empowered to take all the decisions in the household. At the time of India's independence, Jai Narain Mishra donated all his wealth towards social causes and founded the Sri Jai Narain Post Graduate College in Lucknow to help the marginalized sections of society. Therefore by the time Sudhir was born in the late Fifties, his extended family enjoyed none of the opulence that they once had but nevertheless lived a fairly comfortable life.

So, from a very early age, Sudhir was exposed to a variety of cinema. While his father liked watching western films by iconic directors like Francois Truffaut, Frank Capra, Michael Curtiz, etc, one of his uncles preferred what were known as stunt films starring the wrestler-turned-actor Dara Singh, and his grandmother chose to watch the works of Guru Dutt, Bimal Roy and Satyajit Ray. She had watched Guru Dutt's *Sahib Bibi Aur Ghulam* innumerable times and so had Sudhir as many times with her. 'My paternal grandfather was a renowned doctor, one of the first FRCS (Fellowship of the Royal College of Surgeons) from India. He had set up home with another woman and my grandmother (Jai Narain Mishra's daughter) who was the only daughter of her parents, brought up her children in her parents' home. Therefore in a way, *Sahib Bibi Aur Ghulam* was a cinematic expression of what she had gone through in life.

'People often like cinema which is closer to their lives; when they feel that a film has helped them make sense of their own lives, something they often grapple with. It may give them a feeling that the filmmaker has put across their predicament better than what they themselves could have managed to do. They may not remember the stories so much. It's the experience, the moments and feelings that the film evoked in them, the characters and essentially the conflicts that remain in people's memories and not the story as such,' Sudhir offers his analysis of what makes a film timeless and relevant at any given point of time.

As it was with cinema, so was it with literature. On the one hand, if Sudhir read great works of literature, on the other he also devoured several comics as one of his uncles, on the pretext of buying them for his nephew, would buy as many as a 100 a month, and spend a large part of his salary on the purchase.

In the midst of such an eclectic environment, Sudhir's imagination would often take flight and as expected, he began gravitating towards dramatics, elocution and other extracurricular activities in school. He spent a couple of his school years in Patiala, as his father was posted as Reader with the "Punjabi University", and the exposure to North India's diverse cultures widened his perspective further and helped him to appreciate the distinctness in people from a very young age. By the time he came to college, his father had moved back again to Sagar University in Madhya Pradesh where Sudhir completed his post graduation and then went to Delhi for pursuing an M.phil in Psychology.

His life was following a predictable trajectory similar to his father and others in the family. Sudhir was supposed to proceed to Ohio University in Midwestern US where he had got admission to pursue Ph.D in clinical psychology. But during the two interim years spent in Delhi, he met with the renowned playwright and theatre director, the late Badal Sarkar and worked with him on various plays. Badal Sarkar's deep influence ended up changing the course of Sudhir's life and he chose theatre over a dissertation!

It was also around this time when one of his close friends, Vinod Dua, a prominent television personality, introduced him to Vidhu Vinod Chopra. Vidhu, at the time, had distinguished himself by winning the Best Student Award at the FTII and also a nomination at the Academy Awards for his documentary on India's destitute children titled, *An Encounter with Faces*. Sudhir met Vidhu and after deciding to assist him on his first feature film, moved from Delhi to Mumbai. Incidentally, his younger brother, Sudhanshu, after an excellent academic record which included a National Talent Search Scholarship and Chemistry (Hons) from St Stephens' College in Delhi, also decided to work in cinema and joined the FTII. The Mishra brothers made a pact that while Sudhir would learn the craft on the floor of a film set, Sudhanshu would formally study and the two would later complement each other in their respective careers.

After working with Vidhu for the first few years, Sudhir later teamed up with Kundan Shah who was making his directorial debut with a film that has now come to attain a cult classic status—*Jaane Bhi Do Yaaron*—and co-wrote it in 1983. By now, although his hands-on experience with various film directors had helped him tremendously, his brother's course at the FTII had also helped him indirectly to sharpen his cinematic skills.

'I owe a lot to the FTII. In the early Eighties, there was an open and liberal environment in the institute. One could walk into a class and nobody asked you any questions. It was an interesting place and helped me gain a lot of clarity on the technical aspects of filmmaking,' he acknowledges.

After co-writing a couple of screenplays, including Saeed Akhtar Mirza's *Mohan Joshi Hazir Ho* and Vidhu Vinod Chopra's *Khamosh*, Sudhir finally decided to direct his first film and made *Yeh Woh Manzil Toh Nahin* in 1987, and won the National Film Award for Best Debut. A year later, he once again collected the National Award for Best Film On Other Social Issues for *Main Zinda Hoon* and yet again three years later for *Dharavi*.

However a profusion of awards and critical acclaim did not translate into popular success for these films and the reasons were more systemic than anything else. The Eighties were on the whole not the best of times for cinema as video piracy was rampant and the number of cinema-going audiences were fast dwindling. For films that were categorized as arthouse cinema, there were few takers amongst distributors who preferred to place their risk with commercial, mainstream cinema rather than parallel cinema which appealed more to the classes. So even though Sudhir's films were brilliantly crafted stories, they did not witness popular success enjoyed by some of the mainstream cinema.

Reflecting about the prevailing environment in his early years, he says, 'The Eighties were tough times to be. We went through a lot of humiliation. It was tough to hang in. We were treated like a viral infection and tolerated smirks and curt remarks…. "There goes an art filmmaker!" But then, those were *our* times. They were the times we had, the times that were given to us. The alternative cinema of the 70s and 80s truly reflects the India of those days. You can see the concerns, despair, joys, and politics through movies like, *Jaane Bhi Do Yaaron, Dharavi, Manthan, Nishant, Yeh Woh Manzil Toh Nahin, Ardh Satya,* etc. These films played a significant role in influencing popular cinema as well. The poetry of an ordinary face, the sense of reality, strong women characters, all of that found an expression in *our* cinema. What is heartening is today the film community is more appreciative and accepting of that genre of cinema. The children of those who abused us are today looking at us for inspiration! The work that actors like Naseeruddin Shah, Smita Patil, Shabana Azmi, Om Puri, Kulbhushan Kharbanda, etc., did in films like *Mirch Masala, Bhumika, Mandi, Nishant, Aakrosh,* have become iconic amongst most younger filmmakers. They may have forgotten their father's film but still remember *Jaane Bhi Do Yaaron,*' he comments.

Then followed a period starting the mid-Nineties until the early 2000s, which was personally the most turbulent phase of Sudhir's life. Sudhir's younger brother, Sudhanshu with whom he shared a deep personal and professional bond suddenly died in mysterious circumstances in 1995. A young man in his Thirties, with no previous record of ailments, Sudhanshu had directed the television serial, *Kab Tak Pukaroon* with Pankaj Kapur in the lead role and was working on more ideas for television and films when one fatal evening, Sudhir returned from work and was shocked to find his brother lifeless in bed. 'The cause of his death couldn't be clearly established. It was perhaps intense stress, of expecting too much from the self, of living in this big unyielding city of Mumbai. All that possibly killed him,' says Sudhir.

Before Sudhir could come to grips with this tremendous loss, he was in for another shattering bit of news. After his divorce with Sushmita Mukherjee, who had also acted in *Yeh Woh Manzil Toh Nahin* and *Main Zinda Hoon*, Sudhir had married Renu Saluja, the talented film editor, an alumna of FTII and a classmate of Sudhir's friends, Vidhu, Kundan and Saeed. Renu, who was earlier married to Vidhu, was not only Sudhir's soulmate but also a significant professional associate and Sudhir credits her for bringing finesse to his movies through the unmatched "Renu Cut". Soon after Sudhanshu's demise, Renu was diagnosed with stomach cancer and passed away in 2000, leaving Sudhir devastated for a long time.

But as it is said about life and showbiz, "the show must go on" and Sudhir gradually inched back to his craft and his collective pain found expression in *Hazaron Khwahishen Aisi,* which is easily one of his finest films. Set in the backdrop of post-Emergency in Delhi University, the film beautifully dovetails the interplay of love, ambition, idealism and dreams of three protagonists essayed brilliantly by Kay Kay Menon, Chitrangada Singh and Shiney Ahuja. The film not only won Sudhir critical appreciation, it also travelled to several reputed film festivals and won him the prestigious and "mainstream" Filmfare Best Story award.

In 2007, three years after *Hazaaron Khwahishen Aisi*, Sudhir experimented yet again with a completely different genre and made a stylishly wonderful film called *Khoya Khoya Chand*. The film employed the poetic finesse of a bygone era in the Hindi film industry through the story of a young actress called Nikhat played by Soha Ali Khan. Vastly different in theme and detailing, Sudhir's next film, *Yeh Saali Zindagi* was a romantic thriller and the next and yet unreleased, *Tera Kya Hoga Johnny* was about a child who sells tea on Mumbai's streets. It doesn't tire one to say that Sudhir's latest film, *Inkaar* was also distinctly different and deftly explored the issue of sexual harassment at workplace.

Several of Sudhir's colleagues in the industry strongly believe that most of his films have been ahead of their times. For instance, way back in 1991, through the story of Rajkaran, who played the role of a taxi driver in *Dharavi*, Sudhir portrayed how the lives of the poor are impacted by corruption and crime in one of the world's largest slums. Interestingly, twenty years later, Danny Boyle shot in the same location for his Oscar-winning film, *Slumdog Millionaire*. Yet another of Sudhir's films, *Iss Raat Ki Subah Nahin*, which was inspired by a true incident in Sudhanshu's life, broke new ground as it not only captured the drama of a single night but also showcased gangsters as regular people with ordinary human emotions and relationships. It undoubtedly went on to inspire a generation of filmmakers who used the same approach to tell their stories about the Mumbai underworld.

What does he consider more important – popular success or critical acclaim, I ask him.

Sudhir is candid while accepting the fact that it's the desire for success which remains at the heart of every filmmaker. 'Filmmakers have the urge to tell stories and it's a sort of compulsion with them. In that sense, artists play by different rules. They could very well be doing something else but it's the strong inner compulsion to understand life and through the medium of films, tell their stories and connect with a large number of people. What's important for them is to be able to continue to tell stories and popular success helps in that,' he states.

Ruminating over the difference between the older and younger generation of filmmakers, he feels that the younger lot display a high sense of practicality. 'They do not indulge in lament and romanticism as the older lot did. They are open to doing something else before coming back to their art with funds and resources in place. In the world of filmmaking, an artist expects too much fairness and I am not sure whether that is possible. With the general demise of arthouse cinema in the Eighties and the boom in television in the early Nineties, many parallel cinema filmmakers receded into oblivion. Television is a different medium that has its own immediacy. It's a kind of factory where there is no time to reflect. However owing to economic compulsions, a lot of parallel filmmakers took to television to survive. But art is cruel business. You may have to do something to feed your child that may take away your art from you. It's a tough choice whether you give up your art or your child? Obviously you will choose your child over your art. That's where there is a lot to learn from the young. The practicality they have may be a necessary skill to survive in this industry although that ability to adapt to both art and practicality is very tough,' he shares his insights.

On a personal level, Sudhir does not believe in a strict delineation between art and popular cinema, or in upholding the former and denouncing the latter. 'All popular cinema is not bad. There are urges of artists visible in the popular mainstream work of the Eighties. Rahul Rawail was quite interesting and so was Javed Akhtar. It's interesting to see the modernity of women's characters in Salim-Javed films. Smita Patil in *Shakti* was pretty modern and so was Meenakshi Seshadri in *Dakait*. So while there are such instances of modernity and progressive thought in mainstream cinema, on a larger level, the value system of popular cinema was quite bad those days and that's why the alternative space emerged,' he reflects.

Similarly he also appreciates the current trend of casting, which may not synchorinze with the genre of a film. 'This trend is not exactly new. In the Sixties, the popular actor, Meena Kumari was cast as the lead actor in *Sahib Bibi Aur Ghulam* by Guru Dutt. So if the actor is cast right and suits the part, there is nothing wrong in casting a star for a film as that helps bring in larger audiences. When all kinds of films co-exist and when the industry is open to new people and ideas, it's a reflection of good health!' he opines.

Just as he supports and upholds the co-existence of art and commercial cinema, Sudhir also champions the co-existence of the young with the old; the new entrants should challenge the old, while the old should be open to the world of the new. Although he shares a strong bond with his old colleagues-turned-friends like Saeed, Kundan, Vidhu and Ketan Mehta, etc., Sudhir finds young directors like Anurag Kashyap, Anand Gandhi, Shoojit Sircar, Zoya Akhtar and Reema Kagti very interesting. 'I don't have any problems with the young at all. I am also not caught by the tyranny of the young. This world belongs as much to the young as it does to us. Often those who have children tend to live for their children and also get bossed around by them. Luckily, I have no kids and in that sense I find myself free of any chains,' he shares.

To the newcomers in the industry, Sudhir has one message to give and that is about self-discovery: who they are, the uniqueness in their idioms, the indomitable spirit to fight whatever comes in the way of achieving their dreams, and even if it confronts them menacingly at the beginning of their careers. 'Sometimes they may feel the lack of fairness where a big film wants it all and there is no level playing field for filmmakers with small budgets. The industry may lack the democratic norm as there is too much power play by the big boys. If there has to be growth and development, the inherent feudalism of the place should go. But till that happens and norms for a level playing field are laid down, like it exists in the South Indian film industry, there is no point making too much noise about it. It's the same system from which resulted success stories like that of Shah Rukh, Akshay Kumar, Aishwarya Rai, Priyanka Chopra, Preity Zinta, Deepika Padukone, Chitrangada, Irrfan Khan, Nawazuddin Siddiqui, Anurag Kashyap, etc. So one should stop whining and only ask for one's rights by perhaps barging in and by doing as much good work as possible. This place will eventually listen to talent. The film industry is not a closed place. It cares for those who make money for it. Afterall it's a part of the larger society where sons and daughters do have it easy initially but do not necessarily rule the roost always! The film industry in that sense is a more open place than most other industries,' declares Sudhir.

In so far as formal and academic training in shaping a director's work is concerned, Sudhir believes, like most practitioners of the craft, that no one can actually teach someone to be a director. 'The imagination or gift for telling stories, connecting and adding the dots of life to create a story is something very personal and cannot be acquired. However the technique can be taught and FTII has taught many who have made tremendous contribution to the industry. Saeed Mirza, Kundan Shah, Rajat Kapoor, David Dhawan, Sriram Raghavan, Raju Hirani, Sanjay Leela Bhansali, also several directors of Marathi films like Umesh Kulkarni, etc., are few such names. Most of the sound recordists, heads of studios, top notch editors and cameramen are also from the institute. It is undoubtedly an interesting place that has added significant value to the industry.'

And how does our industry look, when viewed from the international context, I ask.

I am not surprised when he says openly, 'We are a nation of mimics. Most of our filmmaking is about following the West, but twenty years later! Technically we are nowhere at par. Look at a film like *Avatar*! Technically, we are still very primitive.

'But as story tellers, I think we are living in interesting times. A lot of original work is happening in the industry. There are some extremely talented people who have an interesting take on life and it's a dynamic place to be in at the moment. With some of the Hollywood studios setting base here, I am sure the rest will also be slowly scaled up,' he concludes optimistically.

In this exciting new environment, Sudhir is busy working on his next film, *Pehle Aap Janab* (earlier called *Mehrunissa*), a black comedy set in his home city of Lucknow, with Amitabh Bachchan, Rishi Kapoor and Chitrangada Singh. Sudhir's eyes light up while talking about the film, which he had decided to make fifteen years ago, and particularly about the casting of Amitabh Bachchan. 'Every film has its destiny. He was ideal for this role and when I approached him for it, he was happy to come on board.'

As always, Sudhir is all set to reinvent himself for this film as well — treating every film like his very first. Dealing with an unfamiliar, new terrain is what makes work exciting for him rather than confining himself to a comfort zone.

So what keeps you going? I ask Sudhir Mishra.

He answers simply, 'To keep working. This is how some people are and this is how they can be alive. I find myself unhappy when I am not working. I fall sick when I go for a holiday. I like taking vacations but only when I know that on my return, there will be work to be done,' he reveals.

With a new film set to release in 2014, Sudhir seems to be coming a full circle from his *Jaane Bhi Do Yaaron* days and I hope this homecoming proves to be a blockbuster commercial success for him.

'Afterall it's (the film industry) a part of the larger society where sons and daughters do have it easy initially but they do not necessarily rule the roost always! The film industry in that sense is a more open place than most other industries.'

PASSION, PATIENCE, PERSEVERANCE

From a beginning in regional theatre to creating a prominent place for himself in mainstream Hindi commercial cinema, it has been a long and self-chartered journey marked with quantum leaps for the very personable Vipul Shah.

VIPUL SHAH

It's that time of the year when the air is filled with the spirit of Christmas cheer and in one of the most pleasant times in Mumbai, I am headed to Vipul's office located at Veera Desai Road in Andheri West. The staircase leading up to his office on the first floor is a virtual gallery, with its side walls covered with pictures from his films. A life-sized Ganesha, carved in sandstone, adorns the wall opposite the entrance door leading to the reception. To the right of the reception, across the glass partition, runs a long corridor with work-cabins on the left. Vipul works out of one of those spacious cabins which has a classy seating arrangement, with intricate tapestry in white and an elaborate dining arrangement at the other end.

Had he not been a rebel, he would perhaps be sitting behind a desk managing his family business of selling books. With an elder brother and a sister, Vipul grew up in Mumbai's Vile Parle East in an apartment complex, a short distance from Parle Book Depot that was owned and managed by his father and his cousin. 'Parla used to be so quiet and peaceful that we could move around without worrying about anything. I was lucky to be in a building which had a gang of kids my age and some who were two or three years older. I had a very basic, middle class but carefree and fun-filled childhood. We enjoyed cycling and playing simple games like *gilli danda, gotiya,* cricket, etc.,' he shares.

Vipul studied in a Gujarati-medium school near home and was a certified mischief-maker. As a child, he had a peculiar approach to academics: he hated the formal way of learning things by rote and was more inclined towards practical application. He would often escape tedious lessons and sneak out from school to either play, or read at the library. 'I must have read all the Gujarati books in the school library,' he exclaims. On the other hand, he was also extremely attracted to extra-curricular activities and won a state-level Gujarati elocution competition for a humorous piece that he had written, titled: "My Mother, On A Strike"!

'I started speaking English only after graduating and particularly after I began working as I realized that most people transacted in English and I felt that a language so widely popular in the country should be learnt. I would listen intently and pick it up in every way possible,' he reveals. As I hear him speak fluently without any vernacular tinge in his accent, I can safely vouch that he must have been a sincere student!

Once he reached his teens, Vipul set his heart on joining the Narsee Monjee College of Commerce and

Economics, because of its reputation for encouraging both dramatics and other performing arts. 'I was clear that I only needed to score 74% in my tenth grade because that was the cut-off for NM to give admissions!' he says. Before every exam, Vipul would visit a neighbourhood video parlour and play games for an hour and then head to the examination hall, and therefore when he secured the desired percentage, it completely astonished his parents, teachers and friends!

With college began his fascinating journey into the world of theatre. 'I started as a backstage boy at Prithvi which meant holding actors' slippers, helping them into their costumes, washing their lunch boxes, packing trunks and loading them on to trucks and so on. I worked with my first guru, the late Mahendra Joshi who passed on his obsession to me and to such an extent that I became useless for anything else,' reminisces Vipul. Most importantly, the applause and encores from the live audience at Prithvi finally helped him to firm up his resolve that he wasn't going to go off stage ever in his life!

However, his decision did not find favour with the Kutchi community, to which he belonged, in which both theatre and films were considered a taboo. Vipul was therefore virtually ostracized and treated like an outcaste for nearly five years. 'My father worried about me. We even had a few altercations but my family was largely very cooperative. My mother in particular, supported me wholeheartedly in whatever I wanted to do.'

Around the time when Vipul was completing his graduation, his family suffered a severe financial setback after his father was swindled by his business partner leaving him with no option but to borrow heavily from the market for survival. In order to alleviate his father's pain, Vipul stepped in and decided to help in a manner he knew best: by producing a commercial play and making some money to repay the debts. He therefore proceeded to borrow a whopping four lakh rupees at a ridiculously high interest rate of four per cent a month to produce the play which was finally staged at the Tejpal auditorium in Mumbai. Equipped as he was with only some amateurish experience, his initiative could at best be described as the audacity of youth. When the play started, the auditorium was filled with 200 people including Vipul's entire family but by the time it got over, only his family remained seated in the hall! 'It is still considered to be one of the biggest flops in the history of Gujarati theatre. That's how badly I started my independent stint,' he laughs in retrospect! But on a serious note, he says, 'I cannot forget the humiliation till date; getting booed and hooted when you went on stage to deliver lines and see people walking out just as you did it—that made me decide, come what may, I will not face this situation again,' he shares.

Not only was an interest amount of sixteen thousand rupees staring him in the face, there was also a deep seated guilt of having created a desperate situation for his beleaguered family. 'I did everything possible to somehow pay that interest back. Those days, regional TV serials paid a paltry sum of 500 rupees per week. I would pick up 2-3 jobs and also some other jobs to ensure that I was able to pay off the interest at the end of a month. That became my one point agenda.'

It is often said that it's the darkest hour before dawn and after several excruciating months of uncertainties, Vipul was finally inching close to experiencing the first sweet taste of success. It came in the form of his Gujarati play, *Andhla Pato* (Blind Man's Buff), which subsequently became the base for Vipul's blockbuster debut film, *Aankhen* released in 2002. Vipul co-wrote this play with his childhood friend, Aatish Kapadia (best known for his television serial and later film called, *Khichdi*) and produced it with his senior colleague from Gujarati theatre, Shobhana Desai. *Andhla Pato* went down in history as one of the biggest successes, unprecedented in any regional Indian language production.

As mentioned earlier, *Andhla Pato* was later adapted for a Hindi film titled, *Aankhen* starring Amitabh Bachchan, Akshay Kumar, Arjun Rampal, Paresh Rawal and Sushmita Sen in lead roles. A fast paced and riveting heist thriller drama about how three blind men rob a bank, *Aankhen* was one of the highest grossing Bollywood films of 2002 and remains on the list of "50 must watch" Hindi films till date.

How did Vipul come up with this novel theme for the play; did the film happen in quick succession; how did he go about casting, particularly Big B. Clearly, I have several questions for Vipul. By now I also know that his candidness as a delightful conversationalist will not disappoint me. And as expected, it doesn't!

I learn that the film happened much later, nearly twelve years after the play was first staged. One day back in the late Eighties, he was watching a film called *Doberman Gang* at home; a habit he had cultivated from his college days of watching a couple of movies every night, which would start playing at 11 pm and go on dill dawn, 'That has still not changed. Most nights I still watch at least one film,' he avers. Meanwhile, he became fascinated with the plot of *Doberman Gang,* in which a pack of dobermans is trained to rob a bank, and wondered if it would be more exciting to replace the dogs with three blind men? He then spoke to Aatish and the two developed it further and wrote the play. In *Andhla Pato*, besides being a co-writer and director, Vipul also played the role that Akshay Kumar eventually did in *Aankhen* while Paresh Rawal played the role of Iliyas, both in the play and later in the movie. 'Paresh used to be the highest paid artist in Gujarati theatre those days and we all aspired to be like him,' Vipul says smilingly.

The play did exceptionally well with over 200 shows running to packed houses and turned Vipul into an overnight star in Gujarati theatre. 'But even during the early days of *Andhla Pato*'s tremendous success, I began to lose interest in acting and found it very limiting. For instance, while performing on stage, I would be constantly thinking about my co-actors—how someone had not faced the light or missed a music cue, etc. I realized that I was slowly getting detached from acting. So I more or less made up my mind that I would only focus on direction and gradually stopped acting.'

In the meantime, Gujarati serials had become extremely popular on Indian television. Shobhana and Vipul lost no time and decided to cast Dr Sriram Lagoo and Tanuja as the lead pair for their debut serial titled, *Chail Chabeela* for DD Gujarat. However, one day when the serial director came drunk on the set, he was dismissed and subsequently the onus fell on Vipul to take over direction as well.

'Those days DD used to sanction only 13 episodes and those were the toughest I ever did! I used to work on a shoestring budget of 18,000 rupees in which to write, direct, produce, complete the episode and deliver it to DD Gujarat. I can't forget how I would shoot the episode at a stretch, from early morning till the time it took to complete, go straight to the edit table, add the music tracks, mix it and from there dash to the railway station and travel in an unreserved compartment, standing all the way from Mumbai till Baroda, reach there at 4-4.30 am and then take a train to Ahmedabad in which I would luckily find a place to sit. At Ahmedabad station, I would bathe in the waiting room and then run to deliver the tape to the studio, and wait patiently till the technical check was completed. Then like a robot I would rush back to Mumbai and start writing the next episode straight away. The profit margins were so thin that travelling in a reserved compartment would have meant wasting money,' Vipul recounts his initial travails in television.

Vipul's creative journey continued undeterred in the same vein and he directed several Gujarati and Hindi television serials and stage plays like, *Action Replay* (later made into a film with the same name), *Mukti Bandhan, Aagantuk,* and *Bhagyachakra*. Meanwhile in the mid-Nineties, when the Hinduja group launched a television channel, Vipul produced *Jeevan Mrityu* for them which marked the first TV appearance of Aamir Khan. Vipul later moved to Sony Entertainment Television and produced a highly successful show called *Alpaviram* which finally led him to his biggest success, *Ek Mahal Ho Sapno Ka* which became the longest bi-lingual daily prime time soap on Indian television to have completed more than a 1,000 episodes in Hindi and 700 in Gujarati.

'We did everything on our own. There was no system of hiring executive producers, creative heads, episode directors, etc. I did it all, both for my TV soaps and my first two films with Aatish. It was only after completing the first 100 episodes of *Ek Mahal Ho Sapno Ka* that I hired a team of directors,' he shares.

It is a well known fact that the daily soap grind is one of the most exhaustive drills on Indian television and involves extraordinary mental and physical strength to sustain each day. Therefore it came as no surprise when one day Vipul Shah, who had produced more than two thousand episodes for various soaps and channels, felt like walking far away from a life that had begun to tire him out. And then by a sheer coincidence, a Gujarati producer approached him to direct a film and it was during the making of this film, which took a mere twenty-two days, that Vipul fell in love with his leading lady, Shefali and married her in the year 2000.

From this point onwards, it seemed as if Vipul's destiny was moving in tandem with his heart. One day he was shooting at the Russian Culture Centre at Peddar road which was just two buildings away from the industrialist, the late Vinod Doshi's (promoter of Premier Ltd.) house. Vinod met Vipul through a common friend and proposed that he should direct a television serial for him but Vipul politely excused himself saying that he didn't need a partner in television but would be open to films and the two parted on this note.

A few months passed and in the intervening period, Columbia Tristar who were launching their films division heard the concept of *Aankhen* and offered to make it but on condition that they would only cast newcomers, at which point Vipul disagreed and the discussions fell apart. Then came yet another opportunity to direct a film for Ram Gopal Varma and Mani Ratnam's company, India Talkies. Vipul began working on the remake of Varma's Telugu film, *Money Money* but due to lack of creative freedom, fell out with him half way through the movie. Eventually, as it turned out, Vinod Doshi met Vipul Shah once again and work began on *Aankhen*.

Even during the days when *Aankhen* was staged as a play, Vipul would often imagine Amitabh Bachchan in the villain's role and sounded Vinod out about what then seemed like a ridiculous idea. Moreover those were pre-*Kaun Banega Crorepati* days and Doshi instantly ruled out the idea as he wanted to work with popular stars! Vipul was however adamant and decided to go ahead with his plan. 'For me Amitji is the ultimate actor. There is nobody bigger than him,' he states.

It now came upon Vipul to meet Amitabh Bachchan. However unable to get an appointment with the Big B, one day on an impulse, Vipul Shah gatecrashed the studio where Amitabh was shooting, and quietly stood in front of his make up van praying for a near-miracle. In restrospect, that seemed absurd to do because Vipul hardly knew the actor except once when Amitabh had come for the trial show of his Gujarati film, through J D Majethia (a popular actor in Gujarati theatre and cinema), and had good things to say about his film. And here was Vipul standing in anticipation in the midst of a teeming media crew who usually followed the Big B! Suddenly the door of Amitabh's van opened and the actor stepped out. Vipul regained his senses when he heard the baritone, 'Hey Vipul, what are you doing here?'

'I had actually prepared my opening line, but he recognized me straight away! For a moment or so, I went completely blank!' confesses Vipul.

He then told Amitabh the intent of the meeting and was asked what kind of a narration did he have in mind? Vipul replied promptly, 'What kind of a narration do you want – 15 minutes, 45 minutes or for three-and-a-half hours?' Since there was some time between shots, Amitabh agreed for the 15 minutes narration and throughout maintained a poker face which confused Vipul if AB was interested or irritated with it! However, at the end of it, Amitabh not only agreed to do the film but also asked Vipul if he could narrate the three-and-a-half hour version? Vipul, who was in an obvious state of excitement, committed to do so within forty-eight hours at Bachchan's residence, Prateeksha at 10 pm!

And here's where the proverbial *kahani mein twist* (a twist in the story) happened! The truth was that Vipul had no script for the film! Therefore, post the meeting he first called Aatish Kapadia with the good news, packed his bags and left for Khandala to finish writing the complete script. Once it was ready, he rehearsed it one last time and landed at Prateeksha. The narration that had started precisely at 10 pm went on till 4 am with Amitabh Bachchan finally saying, 'You can announce it. I am doing the film.'

After a casting coup of sorts, Vipul approached Akshay Kumar who was initially reluctant to even meet Vipul but after being convinced by his manager, finally acquiesced. They met while Akshay was shooting for *Khiladi 420* and similar to the one with Amitabh Bachchan, this narration also began at 10 pm and continued till Akshay packed up at 5.30 am. 'I was going to say no to you but you have blown me off completely and I am doing the film,' said Akshay Kumar to Vipul Shah.

Despite the stupendous success of *Aankhen*, when Vipul came up with the script for *Waqt: The Race Against Time*, he found little support because people expected him to make a thriller again and not experiment with a family drama. He therefore had to wait for two years when Manmohan Shetty, a leading producer and the then Chairman of Adlabs Films Limited, finally decided to fund the film in alliance with Eros and their partnership resulted in several films: *Namastey London* (2007); *Singh is Kinng* (2008); *Commando* (2013); and the latest, *Holiday: A Soldier is Never off Duty* starring Akshay Kumar and directed by A R Murugadoss.

Amongst several others, one of the most significant reasons for Vipul Shah's continuous success has been his exceptional talent for getting the casting right. For instance, he had identified Priyanka Chopra for *Waqt*, after watching her in a cameo in one of her earlier films called, *The Hero* (2003) and cast her with a signing amount of five lakhs. However, the co-producer from Adlabs, Praveen Nischal wasn't in favour of signing a newcomer and asked Vipul to take the signing amount back from Priyanka. Vipul cautioned him that if he did, they may have to sign her for a much higher amount later. And that's exactly what happened. A few months later, Priyanka Chopra's *Andaaz* won her both the Filmfare Award for Best Female Debut as well as the Best Supporting Actress and as predicted, Vipul had to sign her back for thirty lakhs!

Another key decision by Vipul during the casting of *Waqt* was regarding his reluctance to cast Katrina Kaif who was very new when she auditioned for *Waqt*. Even though her mesmerizing beauty was widely talked about in the industry, Vipul didn't cast her in the lead role for two reasons, the first being, *Waqt* was a sync sound film and Katrina could barely speak Hindi and second, the role was that of an Indian daughter-in-law and Vipul felt that however hard she tried, she wouldn't have looked convincing playing it. However, Vipul not only promised to work with her later but also assigned her a Hindi tutor to brush up her language. Two months later, when Katrina met Vipul, she surprised him completely as she not only spoke Hindi, she even read the language and thus landed the lead role in *Namastey London* (2007). Similarly, Aditya Roy Kapur, who was later noticed in films like *Yeh Jawani Hai Deewani* and *Aashiqui 2,* made his debut with *Action Replay* and so did Rannvijay Singh for the same film. 'Every film of mine has at least one newcomer. I like to give a chance to new talent as they bring freshness and energy to the set and shine out,' he mentions.

After *Action Replay* was released in 2010, Vipul has produced films but not directed any. Why has he taken a sabbatical from direction? I ask.

Vipul replies candidly, '*Action Replay* was my first solo production which I also distributed. When the film didn't do well, I had to bear the entire loss. And as it happens, when you don't do well, a lot of people turn their backs on you. It was a big financial loss and it took me time to recover. Fortunately, I am doing okay now.

'There is one more reason for taking a break from direction which in my view is quite significant. A director's life has its own limitations. With every generation, you come under scrutiny whether you are going to be relevant or not. To remain connected with the present, you need to pause, reinvent yourself and then come back. I will start directing after a gap of four years. During this period, I have been writing a few scripts in different genres. *Namastey London 2* is one of them. Then there is *Heartbeat* which is in a different category. There is also a proposal to make *Aankhen 2*. I will soon start filming one of these scripts.

'During these four years, I enjoyed working as a producer and learnt a lot. These days, producers market, distribute and position films and their job is pretty challenging and respected in today's context. It's true that if the director is the mother of a film, the producer is its father. This period has helped me to pause and reflect and I'll hopefully be able to bring fresh insights into my work,' he states optimistically.

The one regret he has in life is that his father didn't live to see him fulfilling his celluloid dreams: he passed away in 1995, much before *Aankhen*'s release. His mother is as loving and supportive as ever of her son and thinks that he works more than he should!

Vipul and Shefali have two sons, aged ten and eleven whom they are consciously trying to keep away from the world of films, at least till they turn adults. Studying at Ecole Mondiale World School in Juhu, the boys have a keen interest in sports like swimming, football, skiing, scuba diving, etc.

With several years of creative work ahead of him, Vipul Shah is focused on creating quality content in different genres under the banner of his company, Sunshine Pictures Private Limited. He is a firm believer in the idea that good content is most critical in entertainment and should take precedence over marketing blitzkrieg. Will Vipul's next film repeat the magic of *Aankhen?* Will it have the desired "pull"? I am sure Vipul Shah will not leave any stone unturned to walk the talk.

'Good content is most critical in entertainment and should take precedence over marketing blitzkrieg.'

THE DISCERNING ONE

ZOYA AKHTAR

In Urdu, Zoya means "to be alive" and that's a nice name for a filmmaker, a profession where one is expected to be sensitive and perceptive. Born to the renowned lyricist, script writer, poet and parliamentarian, Javed Akhtar and child artist-turned-screenwriter, Honey Irani, Zoya and her brother, Farhan were most certainly destined to be filmmakers.

It's raining heavily today compared to the scanty showers in the last few days as I drive towards Zoya's office on S V Road, a short distance from my residence in Juhu and I wonder if I'll make it in time. Zoya has just returned from the Cannes Film Festival after attending the gala screening of *Bombay Talkies*, celebrating 100 years of Indian cinema, alongwith three co-directors of the film, Dibakar Banerjee, Anurag Kashyap and Karan Johar.

The rain gods are unrelenting but surprisingly the traffic is kind and I manage to reach on time. The office of Excel Entertainment (the banner created by Farhan Akhtar and Ritesh Sidhwani) that has produced films by Zoya, Farhan, Reema Kagti and a few other directors, is on the 6th floor of Orchid Pride at the fag end of Santa Cruz on S V Road. As I step inside, I feel an energetic vibe about the place. Young girls and boys are lunching on the open and airy terrace, laden with wooden IKEA-style furniture, next to the reception. At the other end is Zoya's cabin where I find her deeply absorbed working on her laptop, comfortably dressed in black harem pants, with a sleeveless black T-shirt and a grey mélange shrug thrown over the shoulders. I figure later that she has been working assiduously on a script with her good friend and long time associate, Reema Kagti and since Reema is away on vacation, Zoya fits in our meeting.

'My mother was working when we were born. She was a child star. We saw her movies when she was a baby—two and a half years old! Nobody in my generation had animated footage of their parents going that far back,' shares Zoya.

Honey Irani and Javed Akhtar got married after they fell in love on the sets of *Seeta Aur Geeta,* directed by Ramesh Sippy in 1972 (who is otherwise best known for his iconic film, *Sholay).* Soon, the couple had two children, Zoya and Farhan and Honey got back to work when the children were a little older, taking to writing and direction and later even joined the FTII in Pune to fine-tune her knowledge of filmmaking.

'We used to go to Pune and spend time with her. We visited the sets with my father but not as much as the screening rooms. We grew up with other industry kids but pretty much had our own lives. We weren't *"filmy"* kids because my parents are not *filmy* in that sense of the word. So we were exposed to a variety of cinema, different kinds of artists and art works and not just Hindi movies,' Zoya gives me a glimpse into her early life. By virtue of being in the same neighbourhood, Hrithik Roshan, Abhishek Bachchan, Aditya Chopra, Uday Chopra, Karan Johar, etc., are Zoya and Farhan's childhood pals and the comfort levels become evident each time they share screen space.

In due course, Zoya joined St Xavier's College in Mumbai to pursue English Literature and Sociology. 'I knew I wanted to do films but the films really sucked at that point. I didn't fit in. Hindi movies made in the late Eighties and early Nineties weren't my kind at all!' she exclaims. Zoya therefore began her career as a copywriter in advertising but was drawn into the world of cinema after Mira Nair called her to audition for a role in her 1996 film, *Kama Sutra: A tale of love.* Zoya went to meet the director of one of her favourite films, *Salaam Bombay* but explained to her that she wanted to assist her in direction and not be an actor! Mira Nair agreed but on condition that whenever required, she would fill in as an extra and Zoya ended up playing a cameo, as Rekha's disciple in the movie! Although working with Mira Nair was undoubtedly a fantastic learning experience, Zoya consciously chose not to work under a single director and consolidated her experience as a freelancer under several independent filmmakers like Dev Benegal, and a few foreign directors.

Somewhere during this period of apprenticeship, Zoya felt inspired to pursue a course in film production and enrolled herself at the prestigious, Tisch School of Arts at New York University. 'My father wanted me to go much earlier for a full four-year undergraduate programme. But I was having too much fun in life and fought it. Finally when I told them that I wanted to go, my parents were very thrilled,' remembers Zoya.

Although she was at the NYU campus for all of six months, Zoya was focused on honing her skills in cinematic story telling and made several short films. 'If I have any regrets in life, it is that I should have done a four-year degree course. It was an amazing experience to be at the NYU,' she acknowledges.

Once back in India, she continued to work in advertising as assistant director for several indigenous and international commercials. Later, she also co-directed a music video titled, *Price of Bullets* for Pentagram (the rock band associated with music directors, Vishal-Shekhar) and worked with independent filmmakers like Kaizad Gustad on *Bombay Boys* in 1998, and with Mahesh Mathai and Dev Benegal on *Bhopal Express* and *Split Wide Open* in 1999.

Zoya considers her initial years of learning as very atypical. 'I never really worked in a *filmy* set up where I was the 15th assistant and the movie was not going to be sync sound! I have never worked in that kind of a film. I mostly worked with foreign directors or with those who directed big budget commercials. It was a great period of learning; there was no set formula and one could achieve what one wanted and set one's own systems. The only "Hindi-Hindi" movie I worked on before making mine was, *Dil Chahta Hai* and it wasn't really Bollywood because we set it up and made it the way we wanted to. Because I had never worked in a *filmy* set up, it was very easy for us to shoot only in sync sound.' She explains the technique further for my benefit – 'Sync sound is basically recording live sound, so when your movie is done, your sound is also completely done. You may dub some scenes like if it's raining too much and you want the sound to be clear or if it's a scene on a motorbike and the sound is too loud etc. I find dubbing a waste of time. I can't understand it. You are killing performances, it's fake and really boring to dub the whole film again,' remarks Zoya highlighting Excel Entertainment's style of filmmaking.

After working her way through several projects, Zoya finally decided that it was time to direct a feature film and began scripting about the struggles of a young man who comes to Mumbai looking for stardom and success, interwoven with the strains and challenges of his personal relationships. Drawn from a familiar environment, although the story came very naturally to Zoya, it surprisingly took her seven long years before she could actually make *Luck By Chance*. 'It took me a very long time because… nobody wanted to act in it!' she confesses.

Therefore, while the script waited to be transformed into a film due to casting woes, Zoya continued with other assignments. She wrote the lyrics for Gurinder Chadha's film, *Bride and Prejudice* along with Farhan; finalized the casting for her mother's directorial debut film, *Armaan* (2003); worked as an executive producer for Farhan's second film, *Lakshya* and for her close friend from advertising days, the promising young director from Assam, Reema Kagti's film, *Honeymoon Travels Private Limited* which was produced by Excel Entertainment.

Even as little kids, Zoya had always known Farhan to be a performer but after he chose to be a director with *Dil Chahta Hai* in 2001, she was unsure if he would ever take to acting in a big way. However things began to accelerate at Excel Entertainment where everybody seemed to think that Farhan had great potential as an actor and finally, Reema suggested to Zoya to consider him for the lead role in *Luck By Chance*. And from then on, there was no looking back as Zoya signed Farhan even before Abhishek Kapoor (cousin of Ekta and Tushaar Kapoor and director of *Kai Po Che*), signed him for playing the lead in his musical, *Rock On* which released a year before Zoya's film and marked Farhan's debut as an actor.

Even though *Luck By Chance* failed to create ripples at the box office, it brought critical acclaim for Zoya and she instantly began work on her next film, *Zindagi Na Milegi Dobara (ZNMD),* which was not only a blockbuster hit but went on to win several awards including the Filmfare Award for Best Director. In quick succession, a year later in 2012 came an unusual suspense drama titled, *Talaash* directed by Reema and co-written with Zoya, starring Aamir Khan, Rani Mukherji and Kareena Kapoor. Zoya's latest work is one of the four short films of *Bombay Talkies* released in 2013 as a tribute to 100 years of Indian cinema. The film is about a little boy who idolizes Katrina Kaif and wants to dress and dance like her on the superhit dance number, *'Sheila Ki Jawani'* from the film, *Tees Maar Khan*.

I ask Zoya why the four films in *Bombay Talkies* aren't typically Bollywood with the regular song and dance routine? Is it meant to be a statement by the four directors on the changing narrative of Indian cinema?

Zoya is visibly animated by my question and throws me a counter question, 'Why would you want to do the same thing? I am really glad that everybody did something that they don't normally do! Cinema isn't about dancing around trees. I found Karan's film most amazing! It was one of his most honest pieces of work. In *Bombay Talkies*, people's lives were shown as they unfold in reality; they don't have the kind of lives that are shown in mainstream Indian cinema. That's where cinema fits into the lives of real people and something I find very interesting. Dibakar Banerjee and Anurag Kashyap used the opportunity provided by a medium like *Bombay Talkies*, which had a limited budget and time, to tell very effective stories about life. Their stories just blew my mind.'

Talking about her film in *Bombay Talkies,* she elaborates how it was essentially an idea that she had wanted to put across, 'I am a story teller. I want to say things, which is why I am doing this in the first place. I have no respect for people who are putting no ideas out. What is the difference between your latest film, the last film and the one before that? It's the ideas which make them different. I had made *Luck By Chance* and wasn't going to make another "industry-centric" film. What *ZNMD* did was entertain; but it also showcased an idea and made you think about your life. A film should be able to touch you. As a filmmaker, if you don't have a viewpoint and are not able to say how you feel about a certain subject, then you should not be making films,' she proclaims.

Zoya is very firm in her views about what is often peddled as "entertainment" and has no patience for films that are nothing but buffoonery in the name of cinema.

Some argue that films are meant to entertain by any means…, I interpose.

She retorts quickly, 'Someone is lifting up his shirt and shaking his belly—I don't find it funny anymore. I have seen it 500 times! I don't care; it doesn't do anything for me. Why can't a film put out an idea and be entertaining at the same time? I think Raju Hirani says a lot and his films are hugely entertaining. He manages to entertain as well as put an idea into the collective consciousness.'

Some other contemporary directors whose work Zoya finds exciting are Dibakar Banerjee, Tigmanshu Dhulia, Anurag Kashyap, Prakash Jha, Vishal Bhardwaj, etc., and primarily because of their distinct styles. 'I like to see something I didn't know or didn't think about,' she explains.

An avid movie watcher, Zoya practically sees one movie a day, mostly world cinema. So, what about Hindi films? I inquire.

'There are certain filmmakers I don't like, and even if people come and tell me that their movies make money, I don't really care. If it's crude, it immediately cuts me out. It's the intent of the movie that is important for me.

'Only if I hear that the film is different and amazing, a story that is crafty, has good pace and screenplay, has been told well or has performances that are brilliant, I watch it, even if I haven't seen the previous ones by that director. There are certain filmmakers whose work I love and even if people say that a particular film of that director is no good, I'll still watch it because I like to see what the director has done with his latest work.

'For me, *Lage Raho Munnabhai* is so smart, it's charming, cheesy, heartfelt and makes you laugh and cry. I enjoyed watching *Luv Shuv Tey Chicken Khurana* and *Shanghai*. Those were good films but didn't do as well as they should have,' she speaks with complete candour about her likes and dislikes.

So if films are such an instrinsic part of her ethos, does she watch them like a director or like an audience? I am curious to know.

'Yes, I have grown up on films. It was very natural for us… we all loved the movies. My mother had a 16mm projector. I watched *Godfather* on the wall of my living room. Also, one didn't see actors as some glamorous people. They were just regular guys who came home, and hung out. It was so normal to hear them discuss their work in your house; you witnessed how films were broken down in a particular way—why a film was good or bad; why a script worked or didn't, then the reasons for it; a good performance, excellent camera work. So I looked at films from a totally different perspective from a very young age.

'That said, I watch films as an audience. I make movies because I am the audience. I love watching movies which is why I make them. I watch a film and ask myself—am I loving or hating it? If I like something, it's like wow! How did they do it? But all that happens during the second viewing. Initially you are just enjoying it,' Zoya lets me inside her mind as a viewer.

Clearly not one to get submerged by work, Zoya likes to take a good, long break at the completion of every project. 'I really like to travel. I do a lot of that. In that sense, I can't go to work every day! I like to write my scripts and that takes time. While I write and make the film, I am totally there and then I take three months off. I like to visit different countries. That's my thing and I make the time to do that. I may direct lesser number of films than other filmmakers, but as long as my films are good, it's fine. Life is not a race,' she puts forward her musings.

Despite having travelled extensively, she particularly raves about India's magnificence, 'India is beautiful, it's textured, gorgeous and has the most amazing landscapes and offers a vast variety to any filmmaker.' However, there are a couple of aspects about shooting on Indian locations which she finds irksome.

'When you are shooting a film anywhere in India, people don't leave you alone. They just barge into your set, stand and crowd, catcall and stare at you. They think it's a laugh. They don't look at making movies as work. I don't think they have any kind of understanding what work goes into making a movie. I understand they are star-struck and attracted to glamour. All that is fine but can you imagine if a 100 people walked into a bank and stared at the bank teller? That would be outrageous! Can people walk into an operation theatre to watch a surgery? I understand it's done with all good intentions, but it gets very tedious to work. On a good day at a shoot, we work for a minimum of twelve hours. You are on your feet for two hours before things commence and two hours after pack up and that makes it a 16-17 hours a day. I wish people would realize it's hard work and not create additional pressures for us. I like to shoot on locations. I don't like to shoot in studios. *ZNMD* was largely shot abroad so it was okay. But *Luck By Chance* was on locations in India, and it was tough shooting it.

'Besides the actual ease of shooting on location, it's far easier to get permissions to shoot abroad. Unlike India, they have very strict rules. In India you can take a little leeway and do your own thing whereas on locations abroad, you pay and only get what they promise, nothing more or less. Nobody can change that! They are very good with their unions and take care of their crews. When they woo you to come and shoot, they facilitate and make it easy for you. I haven't shot in many states in India, so I don't know what it takes. But whatever little I have heard from my colleagues, apparently it's a nightmare. You have to get twenty different permissions whereas we should be able to seek those in one place! If you go to New York, the Mayor's office has an office dedicated for films and you deal with a single point person. You don't have to deal with the BMC, RTO and a series of offices which can be a big hindrance. You have to *khilao* (offer) money everywhere and they still won't help you. Do you know that in India, specialists are hired in the production team to take care of this aspect and also a security agency for the crew as anybody can walk into your set? Like I said, nobody thinks it's work. They think films are all about stars, glamour and ease which is silly because people in this profession work very hard.

'We hope the government makes it easier for us to shoot as it would make perfect business sense for the country too. Oliver Stone wanted to shoot *Alexander* in India. He left because he just couldn't deal with the bureaucracy. It was a 100 million dollar movie. You can't allow a 100 million dollars to go somewhere else! India has fabulous locations and though people are shooting in India all the time, it would be nice if it was made easier,' she concludes optimistically.

Zoya shares the restlessness of the current generation of filmmakers who demand the world as a platform to showcase their work. To my question, why the Oscars remain elusive for Bollywood, she explains, 'We are one of the biggest along with Hollywood and China and yet we do not have adequate representation of our films worldwide. The Oscars are American movie awards. They have a category for world cinema and they choose films from all over the world. However, it's not just the Oscars, whether it's Cannes, Berlin, Toronto, we don't have adequate representation anywhere! So, why is it that as a nation we make the largest number of films but are not connecting with the world audience? We are content with our own and nobody has been able to crack the code and distinguish themselves. You have to speak in a different syntax for them, in another language. It's not that we don't have film-makers who don't want to do that. We just don't have the producers who know *how* to! If I tell a story to a five year old, I'll have to speak his language; to an elderly lady, I'll do accordingly. So if you are speaking to an audience that has a completely different ethos, your cinematic language has to change a bit. Your film cannot be three hours long, can't have six songs; certain things have to change. That audience doesn't have the need to be spoon-fed with dia-logues that "orchestrate" them how to feel. Those things are cheesy, they think it's amateurish.

'We need to decide whether we want to make movies keeping the world audience in view or not. The point is why shouldn't we be global? We are a cricket-playing nation, and there's huge excitement when India competes at an international level. But when it comes to the movie business, we don't care about the Oscars? It's like saying why do you care about the World Cup. Let them keep playing inter-state tournaments! We make 900 odd movies a year in this country and we must have a presence on world stage. Complacency won't take us anywhere.

'We have a lot of technical expertise here and it will continue to get better as the industry grows.

'Some films made in India—even though with small budgets like, *Bandit Queen, Salaam Bombay, Monsoon Wedding*—did well in the overseas markets. For a film to do well abroad, marketing is a very important factor. A recent example is *Gangs of Wasseypur* which was marketed brilliantly. Yet another, *Lunch Box*, produced by Eros did very well at Cannes and won the audience award. Anurag Kashyap is one director who has managed international marketing really well. He had five films showing at Cannes this year.'

As far as her own orientation is concerned, Zoya plans to make Indian films for the world market. 'That's what I would like to do eventually. But my next film is predominantly for the Indian audience,' she concludes before heading homewards close-by at Bandstand, Bandra to enjoy a late lunch, and on the menu apparently is her favourite Japanese cuisine!

As I drive back, the downpour has turned into a beautiful drizzle and I think about the exciting times ahead for the Indian film industry. With digitization revolutionizing the distribution of cinema, world markets favourably disposed towards Indian cinema and most importantly, a set of enthusiastic filmmakers on the horizon, the possibilities of achieving recognition on the global stage stage certainly seem brighter now than ever before. Will Excel Entertainment be the first to crack "the code"? Zoya Akhtar won't settle for anything else.

'A film should be able to touch you. As a filmmaker, if you don't have a viewpoint and are not able to say how you feel about a certain subject, then you should not be making films.'
